THE ULTIMATE CHEESECAKE COOKBOOK

Recipes from Around the World

Foreword by Giles Coren
Introduction by Judi Rose
Compiled by Michael Leventhal

Dedicated to Elisabeth Ann Leventhal – ML
For Nick Baker – KB

First published in the UK in 2025 by Green Bean Books
c/o Pen & Sword Books Ltd, George House, Unit 12 & 13, Beevor Street,
Off Pontefract Road, Barnsley, South Yorkshire S71 1HN

Copyright © Green Bean Books, 2025
Foreword © Giles Coren, 2025
Introduction © Judi Rose, 2025

Hardback edition: 9781805001614
eBook edition: 9781805001621

The right of the authors to be identified as authors of this work has been asserted in accordance with Section 77 of the Copyright Designs and Patents Act 1988. All rights reserved. No part of this book may be reproduced, transmitted, downloaded, decompiled or reverse engineered in any form or by any means, electronic or mechanical including photocopying, recording or by any information storage and retrieval system, without permission from the Publisher in writing. No part of this book may be used or reproduced in any manner for the purpose of training artificial intelligence technologies or systems.

The Publisher's authorised representative in the EU for product safety is Authorised Rep Compliance Ltd., Ground Floor, 71 Lower Baggot Street, Dublin D02 P593, Ireland. www.arccompliance.com

Edited by Kate Baker
Designed and typeset by Ian Hughes – www.mousematdesign.com
Production by Hugh Allan
Editorial support from Ella Shindler, Tammy Simon, Amy Sussman, Louisa Walters and Anna Wylie
Picture acquisition by Judi Rose
Front cover image: Ed Smith's Honeyed Basque Cheesecake. Photograph by Sam A. Harris.
Back cover image: Silvia Nacamulli's Amaretto and Raspberry Cheesecake. Photograph by Anthony Collard.

Printed and bound in China by Leo Paper Products

Contents

Foreword by Giles Coren		5
Introduction by Judi Rose		6
Nadine Abensur	**Baked Passion Fruit Cheesecake with Passion Fruit Curd**	8
Sherry Ansky	**Biscoff Cheesecake**	12
Bull & Last	**Blueberry Cheesecake Sundae**	14
Mary Berry	**Chocolate Truffle Cheesecake**	16
Martyne Burman	**No-Bake Oreo Cheesecake**	17
Linda Dangoor	**Cream Cheese and Yoghurt Cake**	18
Aviva Elias	**Summer Lovin' Savoury Cheesecake**	20
Becky Excell	**Gluten-Free Apple Crumble Cheesecake**	22
Hugh Fearnley-Whittingstall	**Baked Breakfast Cheesecake**	24
Tracey Fine and Georgie Tarn	**The Ultimate Cheesecake**	25
Badannie Gee	**Burnt Basque Cheesecake**	26
Ravneet Gill	**Basque Cheesecake**	27
Stuart Gillies	**Vanilla and Gingerbread Cheesecake**	28
Galit Goldstein Orlow	**Rose-Scented Mascarpone Cheesecake with Kadaifi Crumble and Candied Rose Petals**	29
Helen Graham	**Orange Blossom Cheese Danish**	32
Ainsley Harriott	**Baked Corsican Cheesecake**	34
Angela Hartnett	**Lemon Cheesecake**	36
Mark Hix	**Dorset Blueberry, Ricotta and Cobnut Cheesecake**	38
Ken Hom	**Caramelised Walnuts**	40
Gil Hovav	**My (Almost) Sin-Free Cheesecake**	41
Ian Hughes	**Cherry Cheesecake**	42
Clarissa Hyman	**Smoked Salmon Cheesecake**	44
Anne Iarchy	**Baklava Cheesecake**	46
Rukmini Iyer	**Chocolate Lemon Mascarpone Cheesecake**	48
Lizzie Kamenetzky	**Parmesan and Ricotta Cheesecake**	50
Kirsten Kaminski	**Vegan Cheesecake Brownies**	52
Josh Katz	**Cheesecake with Cherry Compote**	54
Tom Kerridge	**Baked Vanilla Cheesecake**	56
Sivan Kobi	**Lotus Biscoff No-Bake Cheesecake**	58
Leah Koenig	**Ricotta Cheesecake (Cassola)**	60
Pierre Koffmann	**Vanilla Cheesecake with Red Berry Compote**	62
Kim Kushner	**Cheesecake, Israeli-Style**	64
Marie Laforêt	**Pink Velvet Cheesecake**	66
David Lebovitz	**Cheesecake Brownies**	68

Sharon Lurie	Bobba's Cheesecake with Caramel Apples and Streusel Topping	70
Sarah Mann-Yeager	Grandma Anne's Perfectly Retro Baked Cheesecake	72
Gill Meller	Blackcurrant, Thyme and Goat's Cheesecake	74
Thomasina Miers	Vanilla Cheesecake with Pineapple Caramel	76
Hannah Miles	White Chocolate and Pistachio Cheesecake	78
Monday Morning Cooking Club	South African Cheesecake	80
Yanir Mrejen	Shavuot Cheesecake Made Easy	82
Silvia Nacamulli	Amaretto and Raspberry Cheesecake	84
Silvia Nacamulli	Tiramisù	86
Joan Nathan	Roman Ricotta Cheese Crostata with Cherries or Chocolate	88
Joanna Nissim	Knafe Cheesecake	90
Yotam Ottolenghi	Honey and Yoghurt Set Cheesecake	92
Nigel Slater	Fudgy Lemon Cheesecake	93
Sarit Packer, Itamar Srulovich	Rose-Scented Cheesecake on a Coconut Base with Berry Compote	94
Denise Phillips	Oreo and Raspberry Cheesecake	96
Denise Phillips	Vanilla and Dulce de Leche Cheesecake	98
José Pizzaro	Baked Cheesecakes with Blueberries	100
Claudia Roden	Spanish Cheese Pudding	101
Victoria Prever	Tahini and Silan Cheesecake	102
Judi Rose	Citrus Cheesecake with a Kumquat Glaze	104
Judi Rose	Jewelled Mini Cheesecakes with a Cinnamon Walnut Crust	106
Simon Wood	The Ultimate Gin Cheesecake Recipe	109
Michel Roux	Orange Cheesecake	110
Carmel Sarano	Rhubarb and Custard Cheesecake	112
Sheri Silver	Raspberry Cheesecake Hamantaschen	114
Vivek Singh	Shrikhand Cheesecake with Fennel and Coriander Strawberries	116
Ed Smith	Honeyed Basque Cheesecake	118
Meera Sodha	Vegan Baked Vanilla Cheesecake	120
Michael Solomonov	New School Konafi	122
Marlena Spieler	Classic American Creamy Cheesecake	124
Emma Spitzer	Israeli White Chocolate Cheesecake	126
Rick Stein	Baked Vanilla Cheesecake with Blueberry Topping	128
Adeena Sussman	Boozy Cheesecake Milkshake	130
Eran Tibi	Eran's White Chocolate Cheesecake with Banana Compote	132
Ofer Vardi	Strudel's Distant Cousin	134
Louisa Walters	Jo's Mum's Cheesecake	136
Joshua Weissman	Homemade NYC Cheesecake	138
Itta Werdiger	Cheesecake de Provence	140
Callan Wenner	Ube Cheesecake	142
Shlomi Ziv	New York Cheesecake with Pomegranate	145
Glossary of UK–US Terms		146
Contributors		147
Acknowledgements		155
Text and Photographic Credits		156

Foreword
By Giles Coren

If you had to bake a foreword for a book about cheesecake to raise money for a Jewish cancer charity, you would need, I think, three ingredients.

You would need, first and foremost, around 75 kilos of restaurant critic with more than 25 years in the business, who could bang out 500 pretty expert cheesy-dessert-related words to a deadline, for no money, because he just loved looking at photos of cheesecake. Check.

You would need a spoonful of Jew. Check. Well, I mean, half-check. I was born to parents who were raised Orthodox, I have nothing but pure Ashkenazi blood in my veins and I was brit milah in the traditional way, but there was no Hebrew school, no bar mitzvah, no shul and I married out. So there's not a lot of Jewishness left bar the cheesecake. But that's the important part, right?

And you would need some cancer. Check again. I've got that too. Not a lot of it, just a sprinkling. Prostate, since you ask. Nothing major, just a bit of Gleason 3+3 indicated by a recent transperineal biopsy, undertaken in response to some spikey PSA tests and an inconclusive scan. No symptoms at this stage, no treatment required, just active monitoring. My urologist (I'm a Jew, so he's the best: Harley Street, lovely rooms, beautiful suit) says I probably won't need treatment for many years, maybe decades, but he would be surprised if I do not need treatment eventually. Which is why I have decided to be so generous with my time now, so that there's plenty of goodwill stored up when I need it.

I'm kidding. I didn't know I had cancer when Michael first asked me to write this foreword. I got my diagnosis soon after. I thus feel somewhat of a karmic letdown: you agree to do a good deed for the cancer guys and then when they're handing out the cancers some way down the line, they're like, "Oh, this guy did a free intro to a cheesecake book, we'll give him a pass."

Turns out it doesn't work like that. But at least I got a free copy of the cheesecake book. And what a book! Have you seen who they got? They got Yotam! They got Ainsley! They got Hixy, Nigel, Angela (who did my wedding cake back in the day, carrot not cheese), Tommi, Ravneet, José and Claudia. They got Pierre Koffman, Michel Roux, Tom Kerridge and Ken Hom. Ken actual Hom! I didn't even know he was Jewish.

And what cakes they are. I do not have a sweet tooth, so am not much of a one for cake, which is why cheesecake is my passion. I need the savoury tang of cultured milk to enjoy dessert. I need lactic acid. I need there to have been bacteria. I need a bit of funk. The cheesier the better for me, to stand up to whatever sweet, sharp, fruity drizzle you're firing across it: I love lemon, I love redcurrant, I love blueberry, I love cherries…

And also a little burning. I will eat an unbaked cheesecake, of course, but if you're going to bake it, bake it hard. Bake it till it smokes at the edge. Bake it till it splits. Then go back in time a few minutes and bake it a little less. You can tell I'm not a baker.

But I am a food writer and I am a Jew and I do have cancer. So read the book, do some baking, and devour every cheesecake like it was your last!

Giles Coren, March, 2025

Introduction
By Judi Rose

A Slice of History, A World of Flavour

Few desserts are as universally adored, as endlessly adaptable, or as deeply rooted in human history as the humble cheesecake. From the sun-baked hills of ancient Greece to the bustling delis of modern New York, this creamy confection has transcended borders, cultures and millennia, evolving into a culinary icon that unites us in its rich, indulgent embrace.

Within these pages you'll discover not just recipes, but stories – of tradition, innovation and the shared joy of creation. Whether you're a seasoned baker or a curious novice, this book invites you to explore the world through the lens of cheesecake, one sumptuous slice at a time.

From Olympus to Modern Tables: A Journey Through Time

The story of cheesecake begins not in a patisserie but in the realms of myth and muscle. As far back as 350 BC, athletes competing in the first Olympic Games were said to fuel themselves with a primitive form of cheesecake made from wheat, cheese and honey – an energising blend of protein and carbs. The best of these early cheesecakes were reputedly made on the Aegean island of Samos, Pythagoras' birthplace, where these potent morsels were also offered to the gods, perhaps in the hope that they would grant victory in return. The Roman Empire later adopted and refined the recipe; in his agricultural treatise, *De Agri Cultura,* Cato the Elder mentions a version layered with bay leaves.

These creamy delicacies have also been among the glories of Jewish cookery for centuries. In the pre-Christian era, Jewish communities made cheesecake at the festival of Shavuot to celebrate the delivery of the Torah. For generations, Jewish housewives have marked Shavuot with cheesecakes, their light colour and smooth surface symbolising the Torah's purity and the white robes of priests.

At Shavuot, making a batch of *kaese,* curd cheese, was a way of life for Jewish housewives until mass-produced cream cheese became widely available. As a little girl, I can remember watching my mother, Evelyn Rose, deftly suspending a cone of cheesecloth brimming with milk from an upside-down stool set above a bowl, just as her grandmother had done. By the next day, the milk had miraculously turned into curds and whey. And I can still picture her in our Manchester kitchen, deftly schmearing sour cream over her legendary Velvet Cheesecake before its final bake. "It adds decadence," she'd say, with a wink, "not to mention hides a multitude of sins."

That quiet act of culinary alchemy turned potential imperfections into something that forgives, adapts and ultimately delights.

Over time, it was the Jewish diaspora who transformed cheesecake into a cultural touchstone and an edible art form. Ashkenazi Jews fleeing persecution in Eastern Europe carried their recipes westward. Those who fled from Russia and Poland to England at the end of the nineteenth century continued making their cheesecake with lemon zest and sultanas in shortcrust case.

Elsewhere, Jewish housewives set about adapting local ingredients to create the creamy, quark-based *käsekuchen* that would evolve into the iconic New York cheesecake. The serendipitous invention of Philadelphia cream cheese by a New York dairyman produced a revolutionary cheesecake with the smooth, velvety richness we know today. In Alsace, in northern France, Jewish cooks came up with a savoury version made with smoked salmon and dill, while in North Africa and in the Middle East, Sephardi housewives invented a plethora of mouthwatering savoury cheesecakes featuring local cheeses and herbs, bound eggs and sesame seeds.

A Global Feast
There is a huge variety of cheesecakes from different regions and cultures around the globe – each using local ingredients and culinary techniques. This book is a passport into those worlds. Within these pages, renowned food writers from across the world – from Johannesburg to Jerusalem, Budapest to London – share their interpretations of this timeless dessert. You'll encounter the seductive bittersweet caramel of Basque cheesecake with its burnished topping and airy-yet-creamy interior; or the comforting warmth of a Hungarian *vargabéles* infused with vanilla and nostalgia. For the adventurous, there's an amethyst-hued ube cheesecake made with purple yam jam, or a grown-up twist on a childhood indulgence: a vodka-laced cream cheese milkshake.

Every recipe also tells a story. With its buttery crumb base and dense cream cheese filling, New York cheesecake speaks of deli counters and Broadway lights. Knafe cheesecake, redolent with rosewater syrup, evokes the vibrant and dimly lit coffee houses of the Levant. Even the humble digestive biscuit – a British pantry staple since 1839 – and its US cousin, graham crackers (invented in 1829 by Presbyterian minister Sylvester Graham as part of a vegetarian diet), are elevated to a buttery foundation and compliment for fillings flavoured with warm cinnamon, zingy lemon and gentle vanilla.

Sweet or salty, baked or chilled, these creations prove that cheesecake is less a single dessert than a canvas for imagination.

Beyond Guilt: The Surprising Science of Indulgence
Despite its associations with indulgence, cheesecake need not be an entirely guilty pleasure. The calcium in cream cheese and sour cream supports bone health, and fruit toppings burst with goodness, such as vitamin C in strawberries and potassium in cherries. Even dark chocolate plays a role, with flavonoids that boast antioxidant properties, while the eggs in the filling deliver protein and choline for a healthy brain.

A 2023 study in the journal *Nutrients* revealed that the amino acid tryptophan, abundant in dairy, can boost sleep quality and metabolic regulation. Of course, "all things in moderation", as my mother used to say, but this emerging research invites us to savour each bite with newfound appreciation (and perhaps a little less guilt).

Crafting a Legacy, One Cake at a Time
What elevates a recipe from mere instruction to heirloom? The human hands behind it.

In compiling this anthology, we've gathered not just methods, but our creators' memories. Consider Sharon Lurie's Bobba's Cheesecake, with the addition of caramel apples and streusel, or Sarah Mann-Yeager's Grandma Anne's 'Perfectly Retro' baked cheesecake, which is studded with sultanas and features a delicious lemony sharpness that takes her "straight back" to her childhood.

As you leaf through these pages you'll notice variations in techniques, a reminder that perfection lies in the personal touch. Some swear by water baths for crack-free surfaces; others embrace the rustic charm of a fissured top. My mother's sour cream trick remains my lodestar, but I've learned equally from a Tokyo pâtissier who strains tofu through muslin for 24 hours, achieving a custard-like silkiness. Diversity is the spice of life.

In the end, this book is more than a collection of recipes. It's an invitation to participate in a tradition spanning 3,000 years – and to stir in your own story to share with those you cherish. Whether you're recreating your mother's Yom Tov cheesecake, experimenting with miso-caramel glazes, or whipping up a mini cheesecake trio for a friend, you're contributing to a timeless global narrative.

So, preheat your oven, crush those biscuits, and let the aroma of baking transport you. From ancient Olympians to modern foodies, from my mother's kitchen to yours, the journey continues. And remember: every crack, every imperfect swirl, is just another layer in a rich, endlessly delicious story.

Judi Rose, March, 2025

NADINE ABENSUR
Baked Passion Fruit Cheesecake with Passion Fruit Curd

I live in the subtropical climate of Byron Bay in northern New South Wales, Australia, so I am able to grow a passion fruit vine in my garden. It produces hundreds of yellow passion fruits, almost as big as tennis balls but ovoid and yellow like lemons. So, I frequently make jars of passion fruit curd. Here, to make it more stable, so that it sits without sliding on top of the cheesecake, I add half a teaspoon of cornflour to the eggs and sugar. For this recipe, I have assumed the more readily available, and smaller, purple-skinned passion fruit.

SERVES 8–10

INGREDIENTS

For the base/crust
120g (generous 4oz) digestive biscuits or graham crackers
1 tbsp desiccated coconut (optional)
1 tbsp ground almonds (optional)
grated zest of 1 lime
60g (4 tbsp) butter, melted
pinch of salt

For the filling
500g (1lb 2oz) cream cheese, at room temperature
110g (½ cup + 1 tbsp) sugar
3 large eggs
180g (¾ cup) mascarpone
2 tbsp passion fruit juice from 2 passion fruits, sieved to remove seeds

METHOD

1. Prepare a 20cm (8in) springform tin by cutting a circle of baking parchment to fit and lining the bottom of the tin with it. Preheat the oven to 180°C (160°C fan/350°F/gas mark 4). Meanwhile, have a large, deep oven tray on hand and put a kettle on the boil.

2. Place the digestive biscuits in a large bowl and crush with a pestle or another blunt object, or crush in a mini food processor, to make a crumb with no lumps. Add the desiccated coconut and ground almonds, if using, as well as the lime zest. Add in the melted butter and salt and mix well with a fork.

3. Very lightly butter the sides of the tin and lightly coat with one scant tablespoon of the biscuit crumb, tilting the tin from side to side to do so. Press the rest of the mixture onto the bottom of the tin and bake for 10–12 minutes. Do not allow it to brown. Remove from the oven and cool. Reduce the oven to 120°C (100°C fan/250°F/gas mark 1).

4. To make the filling, turn the cream cheese into the bowl of a stand mixer and whisk till smooth and aerated. Add the sugar and whisk till incorporated, then add the eggs, one at a time, making sure each is well integrated before adding the next. Now add the mascarpone and the passion fruit juice and whisk the lot again for a minute or two, till light and smooth. For a truly silky mixture, pass the mixture through a fine mesh sieve into a bowl.

5. When the biscuit base is cool, wrap the tin in two layers of foil and fill with the cheesecake mixture, smoothing the top with an offset spatula.

6. Place the cheesecake on the oven tray and fill the tray with boiling water, so that it comes halfway up the sides of the tin. Carefully transfer to the oven and bake for 1 hour and 15 minutes. The cake should still have a wobble but not be runny. If it's still runny, bake for a further 5 minutes. If it begins to colour at all, carefully lay a piece of baking parchment over the top of the tin, so that it does not touch the mixture.

7. Remove the cheesecake from its water bath. Then switch off the oven. Leaving the door ajar, return the cake to the oven and let it come to room temperature, about an hour. Transfer the cheesecake to the fridge and allow to set for a minimum of 6 hours and preferably overnight.

Passion fruit curd

Makes 2 jars, one for the cake, one to keep and an extra small bowl for a treat.

INGREDIENTS

For the passion fruit curd

2 large eggs
1 large egg yolk
180g (¾ cup + 2 tbsp) sugar
½ tsp cornflour
200ml (generous ¾ cup) fresh passion fruit juice from about 8–9 passion fruits, strained to remove pulp and seeds and about half the seeds returned to pan
175g (12 tbsp) chilled butter, cut into cubes

1. Prepare two 320g (11oz) jars and their lids by washing in very hot water, shaking out excess liquid and placing in the oven next to the cheesecake until they are completely dry, about 8–10 minutes. Use a cloth to take them out and have them ready just in time for the bottling of the curd, as below. Also prepare two circles of baking parchment with little scissor snips all round and set aside.

2. Now, add the eggs and egg yolk to the bowl of a stand mixer, together with the sugar and cornflour. Whisk slowly at first to combine and then at high speed till the mixture is thick and pale and creamy. Add the passion fruit juice right at the end and whisk a couple of times to incorporate.

3. Transfer to a heavy-bottomed saucepan and place on a gentle heat, adding the chopped, cold butter in one go (despite what other recipes might tell you!). Stir continuously with a spoon or a rubber spatula, going right into the sides of the pan until all the butter has melted and the mixture thickens, about 10 minutes. Do not, for a moment, take your eye off it. The curd is ready when it coats the back of a spoon and you can draw a line through it with your finger, so that it doesn't run when you hold the spoon upright. Immediately remove the pan from the heat.

4. Fill the jars with the curd. Cover with a circle of baking parchment and seal with a well-fitting lid. (You will also have an extra small

Continued overleaf

bowl – cook's treat?) When both cake and curd are completely cold, carefully pour the contents of one jar onto the cake. Refrigerate again for about 15 minutes or until you are ready to serve.

To serve

Run the point of a small knife around the sides of the cheesecake. Release the tin and lift the cake onto a pedestal plate. Then carefully remove the baking parchment if you can. Dip a sharp knife into very hot water so the blade is hot. Wipe dry and cut. Repeat for each cut. Serve and enjoy!

SHERRY ANSKY
Biscoff Cheesecake

SERVES 9–12

INGREDIENTS

For the base
150g (5oz) Biscoff biscuits
100g (7 tbsp) soft butter
½ tsp grated orange zest
1 tbsp sugar

For the cake
4 eggs
170g (¾ cup + 2 tbsp) sugar
800g (1lb 12oz) cream cheese
   (Philadelphia Light works best)
2 tbsp cornflour

For the topping
300g (1¼ cup) sour cream
1 tbsp sugar
1 tsp vanilla extract

METHOD

1. Grind all the base ingredients in a food processor then press onto the base and sides of a dry 26cm (10in) round cake tin.

2. Separate the eggs and whisk the whites with 2 tablespoons of sugar until they form soft peaks. In a food processor, mix the yolks with the cream cheese, cornflour and the rest of the sugar until smooth.

3. Fold a third of the whites into the mixture and combine quickly but carefully, then add the rest, making sure to keep it airy and not to over mix. Pour onto the base. Bake in the oven at 100°C (80°C fan/210°F/gas mark ¼) for 3 hours.

4. For the topping, mix the sour cream with the sugar and vanilla. Spread on the cake after baking, and leave in the oven for at least 4 hours, or overnight. Then chill in the fridge.

COOK'S TIP
- The trick is to leave it in the oven until it gets cold. I learnt the tip from Odetta Schwartz.

TESTER'S TIP
- I used small ramekins to make individual portions, and I bashed the biscuits before using a food processor to make the biscuits finer.

BULL & LAST
Blueberry Cheesecake Sundae

This dessert from the pub's opening menu went down an absolute storm, so we've kept it on and it's become a Bull & Last classic.

SERVES 8

INGREDIENTS

For the blueberry purée
500g (2¾ cups) fresh blueberries
25g (2 tbsp) sugar
generous squeeze of lemon juice

For the blueberry ripple ice cream
2 litres (2 quarts) top-quality vanilla ice cream
120g (½ cup) blueberry purée

For the blueberry compote
600g (3⅓ cups) fresh blueberries
75g (generous ⅓ cup) sugar
1 unwaxed lemon

For the biscuit crumb
50g (3½ tbsp) salted butter
200g (7oz) digestive biscuits or graham crackers

For the sweet cheese
180g (6oz) full-fat cream cheese
50g (¼ cup) sugar
¼ tsp vanilla bean paste or seeds scraped from ¼ vanilla pod

METHOD

1. First, make the blueberry purée. Cook all the ingredients in a heavy-based saucepan over a low heat for 12–15 minutes until the berries have split and cooked down, and the juice has reduced a little. Leave to cool for 5 minutes, then strain into a bowl. Leave to cool completely, then chill until serving.

2. Make the vanilla ice cream base and transfer to the fridge to chill. (*The Bull & Last* cookbook features a wonderful vanilla ice cream recipe, but you can substitute for another vanilla ice cream).

3. Place a mixing bowl in the freezer and churn the chilled ice cream mixture until very thick and fluffy, in batches if necessary. Before you put it in the freezer to set, transfer the thick ice cream to the frozen mixing bowl and put the blueberry purée on top. Fold the purée into the ice cream, creating a ribbon effect (don't mix it in too much), then scrape the mixture into a 2-litre container, seal and freeze for 3–4 hours minimum, to set.

4. Now make the blueberry compote. Put the blueberries, sugar and two large strips of pared lemon peel and all the lemon juice in a saucepan and cook over a medium heat for 4–5 minutes, or until the blueberries are releasing juice (but haven't broken down) and the sugar has dissolved. Remove, stir to combine the syrup and fruit, and pour onto a dish to cool. Remove the peel.

5. Next, make the biscuit crumb. Melt the butter. Blitz the biscuits in a food processor until they form a fine crumb. Mix the biscuit crumbs and butter in a bowl, then transfer to a baking sheet, spread it out and flatten it, and chill for 10 minutes in the fridge. Remove and break the set mixture into chunky crumbs.

6. Make the sweet cheese by mixing the ingredients together in a bowl. Now assemble. Let the ice cream soften for a few minutes, then arrange balls of ice cream with the cheese mixture in your chosen dishes, add the compote and sprinkle with biscuit crumb. Serve immediately.

MARY BERRY
Chocolate Truffle Cheesecake

SERVES 12

INGREDIENTS

200g (7oz) Bournville (dark or semi-sweet chocolate)
2 eggs, separated
50g (¼ cup) sugar
175g (6oz) full-fat cream cheese
½ tsp vanilla extract
150ml (½ cup + 2 tbsp) double cream, lightly whipped
175g (6oz) chocolate digestive biscuits or chocolate graham crackers, crushed
75g (5 tbsp) butter, melted
cocoa powder, to dust
pouring cream, strawberries and raspberries, to serve (optional)

METHOD

1. Break the chocolate into small pieces into a bowl. Set the bowl over a saucepan of hot water on a low heat and stir until melted. Don't allow the chocolate to get too hot or it will lose its shine and become too thick.

2. Whisk the egg yolks and sugar with an electric whisk until light and thick and a trail is left when the whisks are lifted. Mix the cream cheese and vanilla in a separate bowl, then stir in the melted chocolate. Fold in the egg yolks and sugar, taking care not to knock out any air. Fold in the cream.

3. Whisk the egg whites with an electric whisk until like clouds. Fold a spoonful into the chocolate mixture with a spatula. Cut and fold (but do not mix) until no whites are visible. Add the rest of the egg whites and fold in the same way until smooth.

4. Line a 19cm (7½in) square cake tin or an 18cm (7in) round tin with clingfilm. Spoon in the mixture and level the top. Chill for 1 hour, or until just set. Mix the biscuits and butter until combined. Carefully press on top of the cheesecake in an even layer. Chill for a minimum of 6 hours.

5. Turn the cheesecake upside-down onto a board or plate and cut into 12 fingers or wedges. Dust with cocoa powder and serve with pouring cream and fresh berries, if desired.

MARTYNE BURMAN
No-Bake Oreo Cheesecake

I love this recipe because it's quick and devilishly tasty. I hope you do too.

SERVES 6–8

INGREDIENTS

For the base
75g (5 tbsp) butter
150g (5oz) crushed Oreo biscuits

For the filling
250ml (1 cup) double cream
75g (⅔ cup) icing sugar
200ml (¾ cup) sour cream
560g (1lb 4oz) full-fat cream cheese
juice of 1 large lemon

For decoration
100ml (½ cup) whipped cream
small Oreos

METHOD

1. Line a 23cm (9in) springform cake tin. Melt the butter and add the crushed Oreos. Press tightly into the tin. Leave to set in the fridge.

2. Beat the cream until stiff. Fold in the icing sugar, sour cream and cream cheese, and add lemon juice to taste. Next add the finely crushed Oreos.

3. By now, your base should be set. Add the cheesecake mixture. Then put back in the fridge for 4–6 hours, or overnight. When ready to serve, pipe the cake with rosettes of whipped cream and top with small Oreos.

COOK'S TIP
- Pipe the cheesecake mix into bite-sized chocolate cups for a quick canape dessert.

LINDA DANGOOR
Cream Cheese and Yoghurt Cake

This cheesecake is so very light and does not have a biscuit base. You can bake it a day in advance because it can keep in the fridge for four days or more. The topping of almond flakes gives it a nice crunchy texture. You can also top it with roughly ground pistachios.

SERVES 6–8

INGREDIENTS

4 eggs, yolks and whites separated
220g (8oz) cream cheese
80g (⅓ cup) thick Greek yoghurt
180ml (¾ cup) condensed milk
1 tsp vanilla extract
grated zest of 1 lemon
sprinkling of almond flakes, to garnish

METHOD

1. First prepare your cake tin. You will need a 20cm (8in) round cake tin. Line the inside of the tin with parchment paper or use shop-bought 20cm (8in) cake tin liners.

2. Preheat the oven to 180°C (160°C fan/350°F/gas mark 4).

3. Blend the egg yolks with the cream cheese and yoghurt using a hand or electric whisk. Whisk in the condensed milk until very smooth. Mix in the vanilla extract and the lemon zest. Beat the egg whites until stiff, then gently fold them into the egg yolk mixture until well incorporated. Do not stir as this will eliminate the air in the egg whites and consequently the lightness of the cake.

4. Pour the mixture into the cake tin. Cover the top with a good sprinkling of flaked almonds. Gently tap the tin on the worktop a few times to release any air bubbles.

5. Bake for 35–40 minutes until the almonds turn a golden brown. Then, switch off the oven but do not open the oven door immediately. Leave the cake to cool down inside it. (If you take out the cake too quickly, the height will reduce to half and the soufflé effect will disappear.)

6. Once cold, carefully transfer to a serving dish and refrigerate for an hour or so. Serve chilled or at room temperature. Note: this cake will keep in the fridge for at least 4 days.

AVIVA ELIAS
Summer Lovin' Savoury Cheesecake

I wanted to recreate a summer cheese board and salad with Mediterranean flavours. This simple cheesecake is light and delicious.

SERVES 12

INGREDIENTS

For the base

125g (2 cups) ciabatta or sourdough baguette whizzed into crumbs
2 tbsp olive oil or the oil from a jar of sun-dried tomatoes
60g (⅓ cup) freshly grated parmesan cheese
½ tsp dried mixed herbs

For the filling

400g (14oz) full-fat cream cheese
200g (1⅓ cups) mascarpone cheese
200g (1⅔ cups) feta cheese, crumbled
300g (1¼ cups) crème fraîche
1 tbsp finely snipped chives
1 tbsp sliced fresh basil leaves
2 tbsp chopped pitted black olives
2 tbsp chopped sundried tomatoes
5 large eggs
1 tsp salt
pinch of white pepper

For the topping

1–2 sprigs colourful cherry tomatoes on the vine
1 tsp olive oil and a splash of balsamic vinegar
pinch of sea salt

METHOD

1. Preheat the oven to 180°C (160°C fan/350°F/gas mark 4) and line a 24cm (9in) baking tin with parchment paper.

2. Mix all the base ingredients in a bowl then press into the prepared baking tin. Turn the oven down and bake for 12 minutes until slightly brown. Leave to cool.

3. For the filling, mix the cheeses and 200g (1 cup) of the crème fraîche together in a bowl. Add the remaining ingredients and mix thoroughly, adding the eggs last, one at a time. Mix thoroughly then pour the mixture into the baking tin. Bake for 35 to 40 minutes. When the eggs have risen a little and the mixture is thoroughly set, remove from the oven and cool completely, preferably overnight, in the fridge. Remove the cake from the tin onto a flat plate.

4. For the topping, preheat the oven to 200°C (180°C fan/400°F/gas mark 6). Put the tomatoes on the vine on an oven tray, drizzle with the olive oil and balsamic vinegar, add a pinch of sea salt, and roast for 8–10 minutes. Leave to cool.

5. Spread the remaining 100g (¼ cup) of crème fraîche on to the cooled cake, then top with the roasted tomatoes and a little of the oil they were roasted in and serve with a fresh leafy salad.

COOK'S TIP

- If you prefer to make a gluten-free version of this cheesecake, just substitute the ciabatta in the base with whizzed-up almond flakes.

BECKY EXCELL
Gluten-Free Apple Crumble Cheesecake

Gluten-free apple crumble cheesecake recipe, anyone? When you need a dessert that's capable of getting 'oohs' and 'aahs' from both gluten-eating and gluten-free dinner guests, look no further than this beauty. It even has a super simple (store-bought and ready to go!) caramel drizzle for good measure too.

SERVES 12

INGREDIENTS

For the apples

600g (1lb 5oz) Bramley apples, peeled, cored and diced into small chunks (weight once peeled and cored)
80g (⅓ cup) light brown sugar
1 tsp ground cinnamon

For the biscuit base

280g (2⅔ cups) gluten-free shortbread biscuits
85g (6 tbsp) butter, melted

For the filling

650g (2¾ cups) full-fat mascarpone cheese
100g (scant 1 cup) icing sugar
1 tsp ground cinnamon
½ tsp vanilla extract
300ml (1⅓ cups) double cream

For the crumble topping

140g (5oz) gluten-free shortbread biscuits
5 tbsp shop-bought caramel sauce

COOK'S TIP
- If you want to use gluten-free digestive biscuits instead of gluten-free shortbread, use an extra 10g (2 teaspoons) of melted butter in the base.

METHOD

1. Place the prepared apples into a large saucepan along with the sugar and cinnamon. Place over a low heat (stirring regularly) for 10–15 minutes until softened and a little caramelised. You want the apples soft but not too mushy. Drain off any of the apple juices and allow to completely cool.

2. Blitz the shortbread in a food processor (or place into a ziplock bag and bash with a rolling pin) until you achieve a breadcrumb-like consistency. Transfer to a medium bowl and then mix in the melted butter until well combined.

3. Spoon the crushed biscuit mixture into a circular 20cm (8in) loose-bottomed or springform tin. Compact it into the base using the back of a metal spoon then place into the fridge for at least 30 minutes to chill and firm up.

4. To make the filling, grab a large mixing bowl. I use an electric hand whisk or stand mixer for this next part. Briefly whisk together the mascarpone, icing sugar, cinnamon and vanilla extract until combined – about 20 seconds using an electric mixer. Add in the double cream and keep mixing until it firms up a little – this should take about a minute using an electric mixer. Carefully fold in about half of the cooled apple mixture using a silicone spatula. Cover the rest of the apple mixture and store in the fridge for later.

5. Remove the chilled biscuit base from the fridge. Spread the filling on top of the biscuit base and place into the fridge to chill overnight or for no less than 4 hours.

6. Once set, remove from the tin and transfer the cheesecake to a cake stand or serving plate. To finish, spoon the rest of the apple mixture on top of the cheesecake. Crumble the extra shortbread biscuits on top by hand and then finish by drizzling caramel sauce over the top so that it drips down the sides too. Slice and enjoy!

HUGH FEARNLEY-WHITTINGSTALL
Baked Breakfast Cheesecake

The idea of cheesecake for breakfast sounds odd, but this simple recipe is a great way to start the day, especially if you serve it with some fresh berries or a fruit compote. It is incredibly easy to throw together as there's no biscuit base, and you can get it on the table in little more than half an hour. Besides making a luxurious weekend breakfast or brunch, it is also a delicious pudding. If using salted goat's cheese, don't add salt to the recipe.

INGREDIENTS

650g (1lb 7oz) curd cheese or cream cheese, or soft, very mild goat's cheese (preferably unsalted)
75g (5 tbsp) unsalted butter, melted and cooled slightly
3 tbsp fine or medium oatmeal, semolina or wholemeal flour
good pinch of sea salt
75g (generous ⅓ cup) sugar
2 medium eggs, lightly beaten
finely grated zest of 2 small oranges, plus 1 tbsp juice
3 tbsp raisins (optional)

To serve
fresh fruit or fruit compote
yoghurt or soured cream (optional)

METHOD

1. Generously butter a 23cm (9in) springform cake tin.

2. Beat the cheese with a wooden spoon until smooth, then add the melted butter, oatmeal, semolina or flour, salt, sugar, eggs and orange zest and juice, and mix well (feel free to whiz the ingredients in a food processor). Fold in the raisins, if using.

3. Spoon the mixture into the cake tin and place in an oven preheated to 170°C (150° fan/325°F/gas mark 3). Bake for about 25 minutes, until just set, with a slight wobble in the centre.

4. Serve hot, warm or at room temperature with some fresh fruit or fruit compote, and, if you like, yoghurt or soured cream.

TRACEY FINE AND GEORGIE TARN
The Ultimate Cheesecake

This wonderful traditional cheesecake recipe was inspired by our childhood Sunday family get togethers with our grandparents. The tea table was always heavily laden with delicious home-made bakes, one of them always being a cheesecake. We hope you will be sharing this delicious recipe with your loved ones and in doing so, making everlasting memories.

SERVES 10–12

INGREDIENTS

For the base
450g (1lb) digestive biscuits or graham crackers, crushed
1 tsp cinnamon
110g (1 stick) unsalted butter, melted
75g (2½oz) caster sugar

For the cake
2 large eggs
3 tbsp milk
550g (1lb 4oz) cream cheese
75g (1⅓ cups) caster sugar
1 tsp vanilla essence

For the topping
300ml (generous cup) sour cream
1 tsp vanilla essence
2 tbsp caster sugar

For decoration
fresh fruit

METHOD

1. Preheat the oven to 180°C (160°C fan/350°F/gas mark 4) and grease a 23–25cm (9–10in) springform tin with butter.

2. To make the base, mix together the base ingredients, making sure the biscuits are well crushed, and press into the tin. Use a fork to press the mixture down on the base and up around the sides until the tin is well covered. Bake in the preheated oven for ten minutes, then leave to cool.

4. Mix together the cake ingredients, pour on top of the base and bake for 30 minutes. Remove the cheesecake from the oven and allow it to cool for 15 minutes.

5. Meanwhile, make the topping by mixing all the topping ingredients together and pour over the cheesecake. Return the cheesecake to the oven and bake for a further ten minutes. Leave to cool, then refrigerate overnight.

6. To serve, pile fresh fruit such as strawberries and blueberries on top of the cheesecake. It gives it a great look and tastes delicious.

BADANNIE GEE
Burnt Basque Cheesecake

I am a total lover of a cheesecake. I've tried and made a fair few in my time, but the burnt Basque cheesecake is an absolute crowd pleaser, or as I like to call it, 'a real plate licker'. Dark and brooding on the outside and soft and creamy on the inside, it is the modern-day hero of the cheesecake world.

SERVES 12–14

INGREDIENTS

810g (1lb 8oz) full-fat cream cheese (I use Philadelphia), at room temperature
230g (1 cup + 2 rounded tbsp) sugar
200g (¾ cup) sour cream
4 large eggs
18g (1½ tbsp) plain flour
2 tsp vanilla
pinch of Maldon sea salt flakes

METHOD

1. Preheat the oven to 220°C (200°C fan/425°F/gas mark 7).

2. Grease a 20cm (8in) loose-bottomed cake tin. Cut two large squares of baking paper and lay them on top of each other in the tin (at right angles to one another – making sure the corners point in different directions). Crease the paper up the sides so it stands upright – it's fine to have grooves in it as this will add to the rustic look of the cake. You can scrunch your squares of parchment into a ball first as this helps them hold their shape in the tin better.

3. Making sure the cream cheese has come to room temperature, add it to the sugar and whisk together using an electric whisk until it's really smooth and there are no grains of sugar. Now slowly add the sour cream, eggs, flour and vanilla and mix again until smooth.

4. Pour the batter into the lined cake tin. Make sure you thump the tin on the countertop a couple of times with a firm bang to ensure that any air bubbles rise to the top and are eliminated. Sprinkle the flakes of sea salt across the top.

5. Bake for 40 minutes. Timings can depend on your oven and the position of the cake but my rule of thumb for this beauty is that the top should look deeply tanned but it should still have a slight wobble when you pull it out. This goes against the normal cake baking rules as you would never pull out a wobbly cake, but trust me, if you take it out once it has firmed up, you have overcooked it. It needs to be risen like a souffle but still have a jiggle to its middle.

6. As you remove the cake and leave it to cool it will sink, but don't panic. It doesn't stay soufflé tall for long, but that's what adds to its dense creaminess. Once it has cooled, pop it into the fridge to fully set. Serve at room temperature. Slice with a hot knife and eat with a dark, nutty coffee.

RAVNEET GILL
Basque Cheesecake

Perfect for summer BBQs & picnics with a bowl of strawberries.

SERVES 8–12

INGREDIENTS

650g (1lb 7oz) full-fat cream cheese, at room temperature
300g (1½ cups) sugar
5 eggs
150g (⅔ cups) sour cream
230ml (1 cup) double cream
35g (¼ cup) cornflour
½ tsp sea salt flakes

METHOD

1. Preheat the oven to 220°C (200°C fan/425°F/gas mark 7).

2. Beat the cream cheese with the sugar and eggs. In a separate bowl, stir together the sour cream and double cream, then stir the cornflour through the cream mixture. Tip this into the cream cheese mixture and mix well to combine.

3. Line a deep 20cm (8in) baking tin with a sheet of baking paper that's large enough to line the base and come right up over the edges. Pour the cheesecake mixture into the tin. Bake for 45–50 minutes or until the cheesecake is dark on top and puffed up. It might crack around the edge, but this is fine. It should be wobbly in the middle.

4. Remove from the oven and serve warm, or cool completely before chilling in the fridge overnight (your preference!).

STUART GILLIES
Vanilla and Gingerbread Cheesecake

Use ready-made gingerbread as a base in these individual cheesecakes topped with strawberries infused in balsamic vinegar.

SERVES 8

INGREDIENTS

For the cheesecake

50g (1 cup) ready-made gingerbread, sliced
450g (1lb) cream cheese
250g (1¼ cups) sugar
250g (1 cup) crème fraîche
475ml (2 cups) double cream
2 vanilla pods, seeds scraped out

For the strawberries

200g (1⅓ cups) strawberries
2 tsp sugar
2 tsp balsamic vinegar

METHOD

1. Lay the gingerbread onto a tray and leave out overnight to dry. When dry and hard, place into a food processor and pulse until fine crumbs are formed. Set to one side.

2. Place the cream cheese, sugar, crème fraîche, double cream and vanilla seeds into a large bowl. Whisk together until smooth.

3. Spoon the cream mixture into a plastic piping bag and carefully pipe into 4.5cm (2in) deep by 5.5cm (2½in) wide chefs' rings. Smooth off the top with the back of a flat knife and place in the fridge for two hours to set. When set, remove from the fridge and leave at room temperature for 5 minutes.

4. Place the ginger crumbs onto a plate and carefully pick up the chefs' rings and dip each end of the cheesecake into the ginger crumbs. Lightly shake each cheesecake onto a plate, removing the ring.

5. Meanwhile, for the strawberries, heat a frying pan over a high temperature. Add the strawberries and sugar to the pan and fry briefly for a minute, then pour over the balsamic and cook for a further 30 seconds.

6. To serve, spoon some of the strawberries onto the plate, alongside the cheesecake.

GALIT GOLDSTEIN ORLOW

Rose-Scented Mascarpone Cheesecake with Kadaifi Crumble and Candied Rose Petals

Every cake I bake is a song of flavours, memories and love. This cake, with its delicate rose fragrance and creamy texture, honours my roots and the women who have inspired me. The crispy kadaifi brings me back to my mother Berta's kitchen, filled with the smells of her exquisite pastries. The silky mascarpone, infused with lemon zest and rose water, reminds me of Margrit, whose talent for growing blooming gardens and love for cheesecakes inspire me. This cake blends European elements with Middle Eastern flavours, creating a moment of indulgence and joy. I hope it becomes a new song in your home – a song of flavour and love.

SERVES 12–15

INGREDIENTS

For the candied rose petals*

1 rose, separated into petals (all roses are edible, just make sure the rose you selected hasn't been sprayed with pesticides or any other chemicals)
1 egg white with a pinch of salt, well stirred
about 80g (¼ cup + 2 tbsp) sugar
fine brush

* This is optional, but totally worth it. Alternatively, you can use shop-bought candied rose petals or fresh rose petals as decoration.

For the honey lemon syrup

50ml (3 tbsp + 1 tsp) tap water
50g (¼ cup) sugar
1 tsp honey
1 tsp lemon juice

METHOD

Candied rose petals

Brush each petal with the egg white on both sides, then dip it in the sugar till it is completely coated. Place in oven at 55°C (35°C fan/130°F/gas mark ¼) and bake overnight (about 8 hours), until the petals are dry and the sugar has slightly caramelised. Cool and store in a sealed container until use.

Honey lemon syrup

Stir water, sugar and honey in a small saucepan over a medium heat, until the honey and sugar dissolves. Bring to boil then simmer gently for 2 minutes. Remove from heat and add lemon juice. Allow to cool.

Cake base and kadaifi crumble

1. For the cake base, you will need a 20cm (8in) loose-bottomed or springform cake tin. For the crumble, prepare a baking sheet lined with greaseproof paper.

2. Preheat the oven to 175°C (155°C fan/350°F/gas mark 4).

3. In a large bowl, using your hands, separate and tear the kadaifi pastry into pieces. Pour the slightly salted, melted butter over the kadaifi and massage into it until it's completely and evenly coated (it's a bit like washing your hair). Add the icing sugar and mix well.

Continued overleaf

For the cake base and kadaifi crumble
200g (7oz) kadaifi pastry
80g (6 tbsp) unsalted butter, melted
a pinch of salt
25g (¼ cup) icing sugar, sifted

For the mascarpone cream
250g (1 cup) mascarpone cheese, at room temperature
500ml (2 cups) double cream
100g (½ cup) icing sugar, sifted
1 tsp vanilla bean paste
200g (¾ cup) sour cream
2 tsp cornflour
1 tbsp grated lemon zest (about half a lemon)
1½–2½ tbsp rose water

For the decoration
Pistachio nuts, finely chopped
Candied rose petals (optional – see method on previous page)

4. Transfer two thirds of the kadaifi to the cake tin, press firmly with your hands down and slightly outwards towards the sides, for a flat and even layer. Spread the remaining third of kadaifi onto the baking sheet in an even, thin layer.

5. Bake for 15–25 minutes until the kadaifi pastry is golden (keep an eye on it, it can burn quite quickly), then remove from the oven.

Cake base

Gently and evenly drizzle the honey lemon syrup on the hot kadaifi cake base just until it's slightly moist, then let it cool completely. Once the cake base is cold, loosen the edges then remove from the tin. For slick professional edges, after the cake base is completely cold, place an acetate sheet around the baked base (optional).

Kadaifi crumble

With your hands, break the cooled kadaifi pastry into crumbs and keep in a sealed container until use.

Mascarpone cream

1. Place the mascarpone cheese in the bowl of a stand mixer and beat for 2 minutes on medium speed, until the mascarpone is smooth. Add the double cream, sifted icing sugar and vanilla bean paste, and then whisk to form soft peaks.

2. In another bowl, mix the sour cream, cornflour, lemon zest and rose water (at first add 1½ tablespoons and keep on adding if needed). Mix well. Gently fold the mascarpone cream into the sour cream mixture until it is fully combined.

Assemble the cake

Spread the rose-scented mascarpone cream over the kadaifi base and level it. Place in the refrigerator overnight to set. (If you used the acetate sheet around the base, place the cake in the freezer for 2 more hours and only then remove it, in order to get the perfect clean edges). Sprinkle the kadaifi crumble and decorate with finely chopped pistachio nuts and rose pedals (optional).

HELEN GRAHAM
Orange Blossom Cheese Danish

My favourite baked good is without doubt a cheese Danish pastry – essentially a cheesecake bun, always with an inappropriate amount of icing sugar that would invariably precede a sneezing fit. This is my version, using shop-bought puff. The addition of orange blossom in the cheesecake mix and toasted sesame seeds makes these really special.

SERVES 6

INGREDIENTS

320g (11oz) ready-rolled puff pastry sheet

For the egg wash
1 large egg, beaten with 1 tsp water

For the filling
230g (1⅓ cup) ricotta
1 egg yolk
2 tbsp icing sugar, plus more for garnish
½ tbsp lemon juice
1 tbsp orange blossom water
¼ tsp Maldon sea salt
zest of 1 lemon
1½ tbsp toasted sesame seeds

For the glaze
2 tbsp honey/agave syrup
1 tsp orange blossom water

METHOD

1. Preheat the oven to 180°C (160°C fan/350°F/gas mark 4).

2. Unroll your pastry and cut into 6 equal squares: cut in half horizontally, and then cut into three vertically. With each square, fold the corners into the middle. Transfer these to a lined baking tray and brush each square lightly with the egg wash.

3. Whisk together all the ingredients for the filling (apart from the sesame seeds) until fully combined. Spoon the filling onto the middle of each square, dividing the mix equally. Sprinkle over the sesame seeds and then bake for 20 minutes until golden brown.

4. Make the glaze by combining the honey with the orange blossom. While the pastries are still hot, drizzle over the glaze, then sift over a little icing sugar.

AINSLEY HARRIOTT
Baked Corsican Cheesecake

This is a really easy, zesty gluten-free Corsican dessert that's a cross between a flan and a baked cheesecake. On the island, they have a local liqueur called 'myrtle eau de vie', made from the berries of the myrtle shrub, which has a very distinct and slightly aromatic flavour. If you can find some, then do use it to add a unique flavour; otherwise, use limoncello for a delicate lemony treat.

SERVES 6–8

INGREDIENTS
butter or vegetable oil, for greasing
500g (3 cups) ricotta cheese (or brocciu/brousse cheese, if you can get it)
140g (scant ¾ cup) sugar
2 large unwaxed lemons, zest only
4 eggs
1 tbsp myrtle liqueur/eau de vie, limoncello or grappa
mixed fresh berries, to serve

METHOD

1. Preheat the oven to 180°C (160°C fan/350°F/gas mark 4). Lightly grease a 20cm (8in) springform cake tin and line the bottom with baking parchment.

2. Strain off any excess liquid from the ricotta by placing it in a sieve over a bowl for 20–30 minutes. Once strained, place the cheese in a mixing bowl and break it down using a fork. Add 40g (3 tablespoons + 1 teaspoon) of the sugar and the lemon zest and mix well.

3. In a separate bowl, use an electric hand mixer to whisk the eggs with the remaining sugar for 4–6 minutes until pale, fluffy and tripled in volume. Slowly add the egg mixture, a little at a time, to the ricotta mixture, gently folding it in, making sure to keep as much air in the mixture as possible. Do not over mix. Add the liqueur and gently mix in.

4. Pour the mixture into the cake tin and bake for 40–45 minutes or until the top is lightly golden and set, but still with a very slight wobble. It will firm up as it cools. Leave to completely cool in the tin before turning out onto a serving plate, then chill before cutting into slices and serving with fresh berries.

TESTER'S TIP
This works beautifully topped with lemon zest and honey.

ANGELA HARTNETT
Lemon Cheesecake

The beauty of lemons is their versatility; they can brighten both savoury and sweet dishes. This easy cheesecake stars a zesty topping and you can team it with extra citrus in the form of orange slices or segments to serve.

SERVES 6–8

INGREDIENTS

For the base
75g (5 tbsp) butter
175g (6oz) digestive biscuits or graham crackers
50g (½ cup) ground almonds

For the filling
100g (3½oz) full-fat cream cheese
250g (1 cup) mascarpone
80g (½ cup) icing sugar
zest of 1 lemon
juice of 2 lemons

To serve
Blood orange slices or segments, or poached rhubarb

METHOD

1. Line the base and sides of a 20cm (8in) loose-bottomed cake tin with baking parchment.

2. To make the base, melt the butter in a saucepan over a low heat. Crush the digestive biscuits under baking parchment or in a mixing bowl, using the end of a rolling pin, until you have a powdery rubble. Stir in the ground almonds and melted butter until fully combined, then press the mixture into the bottom of the cake tin. Place in the fridge to firm up while you make the filling.

3. Cream together the cream cheese, mascarpone and icing sugar, then beat in the lemon zest and juice, mixing well to combine.

4. Take the base out of the fridge (it should be firmer by now) and top with the cheesecake mixture, smoothing the surface to ensure a nice, even top. Place back in the fridge for at least two hours to set.

5. Serve with blood orange slices or segments, or poached rhubarb.

MARK HIX
Dorset Blueberry, Ricotta and Cobnut Cheesecake

SERVES 6–8

INGREDIENTS

For the blueberry syrup
450g (2½ cups) blueberries
200g (1 cup) sugar
200ml (¾ cup + 1 tbsp) water
20g (2 tbsp + 2 tsp) cornflour

For the base
250g (9oz) digestive biscuits, graham crackers or Hobnob biscuits
80g (5½ tbsp) butter, melted

For the filling
300ml (1¼ cups) double cream
100g (½ cup) sugar
250g (9oz) cream cheese, softened to room temperature
250g (1½ cups) ricotta, softened to room temperature
finely grated zest of 1 lemon
1 tsp vanilla extract
120–150g (¾–1 cup) cobnuts or hazelnuts, lightly toasted

METHOD

1. Put 200g (generous 1 cup) of the blueberries (use the softer ones) into a pan with the sugar and 175ml (¾ cup) water. Slowly bring to the boil to dissolve the sugar, then simmer for 3–4 minutes. Mix the cornflour with the remaining water and add to the pan, stirring. Simmer, still stirring, for another 2–3 minutes. Remove from the heat and strain through a fine sieve into a bowl, pushing the berries in the sieve with the back of a spoon to extract as much juice as possible. Leave to cool.

2. Meanwhile, line a 17–18cm (7in) round springform cake tin with greaseproof paper. Crush the biscuits in a food processor until they are the texture of coarse breadcrumbs – or you can smash them in a plastic bag with a rolling pin. Mix the biscuit crumbs with the melted butter and pack into the cake tin, firming down with the back of a spoon.

3. Whip the cream and sugar together until fairly stiff. In another bowl, beat the cream cheese and ricotta until it softens a little, then fold in the whipped cream with the lemon zest and vanilla extract. Lightly fold through half of the cooled blueberry syrup (don't mix too thoroughly, though, as you want a ripple effect) along with half of the cobnuts, roughly chopped. Spoon the mix on to the biscuit base and place in the fridge for 2–3 hours, or overnight, until firm.

4. When ready to serve, mix the rest of the blueberries with the remaining blueberry syrup. To take the cheesecake out, run a hot knife around the edge, then release the side of the tin and slide the cheesecake on to a board. Cut into slices and serve each portion topped with a couple of spoonfuls of the blueberry sauce and either whole or lightly chopped cobnuts.

KEN HOM
Caramelised Walnuts

The first time I had this delicious snack was in Beijing and I was determined to learn how to make them. As it turned out, they were surprisingly easy. The shelled walnuts must be blanched first to rid them of any bitterness. They are then rolled in sugar, left to dry for several hours, then deep-fried to caramelise the sugar coating. Finally, they are rolled in sesame seeds. The result is a classic contrast of tastes and textures.

(We selected this recipe by Ken Hom because these caramelised walnuts make a wonderfully sweet, nutty and luxurious cheesecake topping. Just add to your cheesecake of choice before serving.)

SERVES 4

INGREDIENTS

225g (2 cups) walnuts, shelled
100g (½ cup) sugar
450ml (1¾ cups + 2 tbsp) groundnut or vegetable oil
3 tbsp sesame seeds

METHOD

1. Bring a pot of water to the boil. Add the walnuts and cook for about 10 minutes to blanch them. Drain the nuts in a colander or sieve, then pat dry with kitchen paper and spread them on a baking tray.

2. Sprinkle the sugar over the walnuts and roll them around in the sugar to cover them completely. Place the tray of sugared walnuts in a cool, draughty place. Let them dry for at least 2 hours, preferably overnight. (The recipe can be done ahead to this point.)

3. Heat the oil in a deep-fat fryer or wok to a moderate heat. Fry a batch of the walnuts for about 2 minutes or until the sugar melts and the walnuts turn golden. (Watch the heat to prevent burning.)

4. Remove the walnuts from the oil with a slotted spoon or strainer. Sprinkle them with some of the sesame seeds and lay them on a nonstick baking tray or a cake rack to cool. (Do not drain them on kitchen paper as the sugar will stick when it dries.) Deep-fry and drain the rest of the walnuts in the same way.

5. Cooled, the caramel walnuts can be kept in a sealed glass jar for about 2 weeks. Serve them warm or cold.

GIL HOVAV
My (Almost) Sin-Free Cheesecake

For years I have been trying to come up with a good recipe for a diet cheesecake. This one is my best shot. It has a few tricks: for instance, nobody likes the taste of artificial sweeteners, but lime zest and juice can hide it really well. The texture (and taste) of light cream cheese also leave something to be desired, but mixed with cinnamon and nuts it is really good! Try it and thank me later.

INGREDIENTS
- 340g (2 cups) shelled nuts (I prefer hazelnuts, but walnuts, pecan and even almonds are fine)
- 1 scant tsp cinnamon
- 1 egg white
- 500g (1lb 2oz) light cream cheese
- 1 egg
- 1 egg yolk
- 100g (½ cup) sugar substitute such as xylitol
- zest of 2 limes
- juice of 1 lime
- 400g (1½ cups) light sour cream

METHOD
1. Put nuts, cinnamon and egg white in the food processor. Process until the mixture looks like breadcrumbs. Transfer to a rectangle 20cm x 30cm (8in x 12in) Pyrex dish, press and flatten.

2. Put all the rest of the ingredients (except for the sour cream) in the food processor (no need to wash) and mix. Pour into the baking dish on top of the nut mixture.

3. Bake in a 180°C (160°C fan/350°F/gas mark 4) oven for 40 minutes, until the edges start to become golden and the cake is firm. Smear sour cream on top and bake for another 15 minutes. Let cool to room temperature and then keep in the fridge.

IAN HUGHES
Cherry Cheesecake

While working on the design of this book, I rather cheekily sent the publisher this recipe to try out. He made it, decided it was really delicious, and said it had to be included! It is very quick and easy to put together and perfect when the cherries come into season at the beginning of June.

SERVES 6

INGREDIENTS

200g (7oz) digestive biscuits or graham crackers, crushed to crumb texture
85g (6 tbsp) butter, melted but cooled off a bit
700–750g (5–5 ⅓ cups) cherries, stones removed
5 tbsp (70g) sugar
4 tbsp kirsch
2 egg yolks
250ml (1 cup) double cream
250g (1 cup) mascarpone cheese
3–4 chocolate flake bars
a few chopped hazelnuts to decorate

METHOD

1. Grease and line the bottom of a 20cm (8in) springform cake tin.

2. Put the crushed biscuits in a bowl, add the butter and mix well until thoroughly coated. Tip into the tin and compact it with a wooden spoon or palette knife, then place it into the fridge for 30 minutes to firm up.

3. Put the de-stoned cherries, 3 tablespoons of sugar and 2 tablespoons of kirsch in a pan and heat gently over a medium heat until the sugar has dissolved and the cherry skins are just starting to split. This will take around 5–10 minutes. Remove from the heat and leave to cool.

4. In a clean mixing bowl, add the egg yolks and 2 tablespoons of sugar. Give it a good whisk until the colour changes from yellow to a pale cream. Pour in the cream and beat until it forms soft peaks, then mix it with the mascarpone and 2 tablespoons of kirsch until combined to a smooth, creamy mixture that holds its shape.

5. Scatter the cooled cherries evenly over the biscuit base, crumble the flake bars over the top, then cover with the thick, creamy mixture.

6. Place the cheesecake in the fridge for at least 2 hours and, when ready to serve, sprinkle with some chopped hazelnuts.

CLARISSA HYMAN
Smoked Salmon Cheesecake

I grew up in a Jewish deli – raised in a pickle barrel, my mother would sometimes say. My father used to slice our home-smoked salmon as if he were Isaac Stern playing the violin, in between dispensing 'Jewish lollipops' – small slices of salmon – to the kids from King David School crowding the shop after school. I always hated the stuff when I was young; now, of course, when I have to pay for it just like everyone else, I find I really like it after all. When my mother was in hospital, I knew she was on the mend when she managed to say, faintly but clearly, that maybe, just maybe, she could manage a little smoked salmon sandwich. They would have both enjoyed this retro recipe which enjoyed a certain vogue some years ago. It's pretty rich and a little goes a long way, so it makes a useful buffet standby. Serve with a green salad and – what else? – buttered bagels.

SERVES 8

INGREDIENTS
butter, for greasing
50g (1 cup) fine dried breadcrumbs
50g (½ cup) grated Parmesan
350g (12½oz) cream cheese
350g (12½oz) curd cheese
250ml (1 cup) sour cream
juice of 1 lemon (about 3 tbsp)
3 large eggs
20g (¾ cup) fresh dill, finely chopped
plenty of freshly ground black pepper
salt
125g (4½oz) smoked salmon, flaked (use a mild, buttery salmon not one with a strong, oaky cure)
dill sprigs and thinly sliced lemon, to decorate

METHOD

1. Preheat the oven to 180°C (160°C fan/350°F/gas mark 4). Butter the bottom and sides of a 20cm (8in) round springform tin.

2. Mix the breadcrumbs and grated Parmesan. Add to the tin; tilt, shake and turn until the sides are covered, then gently press the remaining crumbs over the bottom to make a thick crust. Leave in the fridge until ready to bake.

3. Beat the cream and curd cheeses till smooth (most easily done in a mixer fitted with a paddle blade), then stir in the sour cream and lemon juice. Mix in the eggs one by one. Next, add the dill, plenty of black pepper and a little salt. Then fold in the smoked salmon.

4. Pour the mixture into the prepared tin and bake for 45 minutes. Turn off the heat and leave in the cooling oven for another hour. Remove, cool and refrigerate overnight or for several hours.

5. Before serving, decorate with sprigs of dill and thin slices of lemon.

ANNE IARCHY
Baklava Cheesecake

If you're a lover of baklava and cheesecake, this cake is for you. I like to use Polish cream cheese as opposed to Philadelphia as it's slightly smoother. You can adapt the sweetness of the cake by adding the full amount or slightly less of the simple sugar. The rose petals do add that special flavour as well as colour. Note: this cake needs to be prepared a day ahead.

SERVES 8–10

INGREDIENTS

For the simple syrup
120g (½ cup + 2 tbsp) sugar
120ml (½ cup) water

For the cake
120g (8 tbsp) melted unsalted butter
10 sheets of filo pastry
150g (1½ cups) crushed pistachio kernels
12g (1 tbsp) sugar
500g (1lb 2oz) cream cheese
200g (1 cup) sugar
4 medium eggs
1 tbsp vanilla
25g (¼ cup) plain flour
225ml (scant cup) double cream

For the decoration
handful of rose petals
handful of the crushed pistachio kernels

METHOD

1. To make the simple syrup: dissolve the sugar in the water while heating over a low heat in a heavy-bottomed saucepan. Bring to the boil, then switch off the heat and leave to cool. You might not need all of the syrup. The rest can be stored in a clean empty jam jar in the fridge for up to 4 weeks.

2. Preheat the oven to 190°C (170°C fan/375°F/gas mark 5) and line the bottom and sides of a 20cm (8in) springform cake tin with parchment paper.

3. Brush 6 tablespoons of the melted butter generously on eight sheets of filo pastry and layer them across one another horizontally and vertically to cover the base and sides of the tin. Naturally, there will be a gap or well formed, where later we'll be pouring the cheesecake mixture into. Bake for 10 minutes.

4. Set aside a handful of pistachios for decorating at the end. Mix the remainder with 1 tablespoon of sugar and 1 tablespoon of melted butter in a small bowl. In a stand mixer (or with a hand mixer), cream the cheese and 200g (1 cup) of sugar until soft, add the eggs one by one and the vanilla until well combined. Add the flour and the double cream and mix. The mixture will be quite runny.

5. On the baked base, add the pistachio mix and press down on the pastry. Don't worry if you hear the crushing noise of the breaking pastry. Pour the cream cheese mixture on top of the pistachio mixture. Pour it as much as you can into the centre of the pastry base, as it can tend to seep out of the sides.

6. Crinkle the remaining two filo pastry sheets and press them onto the cream cheese mixture. Brush the top with the rest of the melted butter. Bake for 50 minutes until golden. If the cake is getting too dark, cover with some foil. Once out of the oven, drizzle with about 60–80ml (½ cup) of the simple syrup and sprinkle with the rose petals and remaining pistachios. Allow to cool at room temperature then place in the fridge for 8 hours or overnight.

RUKMINI IYER
Chocolate Lemon Mascarpone Cheesecake

SERVES 8

INGREDIENTS

150g (5oz) chocolate digestive biscuits or chocolate graham crackers

60g (4 tbsp) unsalted butter, melted

250g (1 cup) mascarpone cheese, at room temperature

250g (9oz) full-fat Philadelphia cheese, at room temperature

300g (10oz) dark chocolate (70% cocoa solids)

25g (1 tbsp + 1 tsp) honey

150g (½ cup) lemon curd

METHOD

1. Blitz the digestive biscuits in a food processor (or smash them in a bag, using a rolling pin) until fine. Mix with the melted butter, then pat down evenly over the lined base of a 20cm (8in) springform cake tin. Transfer to the fridge to set.

2. Whisk the mascarpone and Philadelphia together until smooth and set aside. Melt the dark chocolate in a heatproof bowl and set over a pan of simmering water (don't let the base of the bowl touch the boiling water). Turn off the heat.

3. Whisk 2 heaped tablespoons of the mascarpone mix into the chocolate; once incorporated, add the rest a few tablespoons at a time, along with the honey, until smoothly mixed: do this quite quickly, as the chocolate will want to set – a vigorous beating will bring it all together smoothly.

4. Spread the lemon curd all over the chilled biscuit base, then add heaped tablespoons of the chocolate mixture over the top and smooth it down evenly. Return the tin to the fridge to set overnight.

5. To unmould, carefully run a hot knife around the edges of the springform tin, then remove the sides. Let the cheesecake sit for 10 minutes at room temperature before serving.

LIZZIE KAMENETZKY
Parmesan and Ricotta Cheesecake

I confess that I don't really understand cheesecake as a dessert – not that I dislike it, it just doesn't fill me with the same joy that others seem to get. A savoury cheesecake, on the other hand, is something that I can really get behind. As well as making a first-class lunch with a salad it also makes a different and exciting end to a meal, a cheese course in a different form.

SERVES 8–10

INGREDIENTS
100g (7 tbsp) unsalted butter, melted, plus extra to grease
125g (4oz) oatcakes
75g (2½oz) digestive biscuits or graham crackers
25g (¼ cup) shelled walnuts
300g (10oz) full-fat cream cheese
300g (1¼ cups) ricotta
150g (1½ cups) grated parmesan (or vegetarian alternative)
4 medium free-range eggs
small bunch fresh chives, snipped
black pepper, to taste

METHOD
1. Preheat the oven to 150°C (130°C fan/300°F/gas mark 2) and grease a 20cm (8in) loose-bottomed or springform cake tin.

2. Whizz the oatcakes, biscuits and walnuts into fine crumbs in a food processor (or crush finely in a large freezer bag with a rolling pin). Put in a bowl, then add the melted butter and mix until it looks like wet sand. Press into the base of the tin, working it to the edges and a little up the sides. Chill for at least 30 minutes.

3. In a large bowl, beat the cream cheese, ricotta and parmesan (or alternative) until smooth using an electric mixer. Beat in the eggs and chives, then season with plenty of freshly ground black pepper.

4. Pour the cheese mixture onto the chilled biscuit base, then bake for 50–60 minutes until it's set, with a slight wobble in the centre. Cool fully in the tin, then remove to serve.

KIRSTEN KAMINSKI
Vegan Cheesecake Brownies

Vegan Cheesecake Brownies. Do I need to say more? I literally can't imagine anyone not liking these delicious squares. They combine the best out of two popular desserts. Ooey-gooey chocolate brownies and smooth, rich cheesecake! Yum! These Vegan Cheesecake Brownies are just worth making, as they're really simple and quick to prepare but are absolutely mouthwatering!

SERVES 9

INGREDIENTS

Brownies layer

125g (1 cup) plain flour
28g (⅓ cup) cacao powder
65g (⅓ cup) coconut sugar
½ tsp baking powder
pinch of salt
120g (4oz) dark vegan chocolate, melted
60ml (⅓ cup) vegan butter/coconut oil, melted
½ tsp vanilla extract
⅓ cup almond butter
80ml (½ cup) soy/almond milk

Cheesecake layer

240ml (1 cup) vegan yogurt
½ cup cashews, soaked
1 tbsp cornflour

Toppings

85g (½ cup) vegan chocolate chips

METHOD

1. Preheat the oven to 175°C (155°C fan/350°F/gas mark 4)

2. Place the flour, cacao powder, coconut sugar, baking powder and salt in a medium size bowl and whisk together. Melt the chocolate and add the butter, vanilla extract, almond butter and milk to it. Whisk together until you have a smooth mixture, then add to the dry ingredients. Combine with a spatula and set aside.

3. Place the cashews, vegan yogurt and cornflour into a high-speed blender and blend for 30 seconds until smooth.

3. Line a 20cm (8in) brownie tin with parchment paper and grease the sides. Scoop half of the brownie batter into the tin and spread evenly. Add the cheesecake mixture on top and even out carefully. Add the remaining half of the batter on top and use a toothpick or fork to create swirls.

4. Sprinkle chocolate chips on top and place in the oven for 35–40 minutes (depending on how gooey you want them). Allow to cool down for 5–10 minutes before cutting and serving.

JOSH KATZ
Cheesecake with Cherry Compote

SERVES 12 generously

INGREDIENTS

For the cheesecake crumb

187g (¾ cup + 3 tbsp) dark brown sugar
150g (¾ cup) sugar
40g (2 tbsp) honey
4g (1 tsp) fine salt
455g (4 sticks) unsalted butter, softened
640g (4 cups) plain flour
10g (1½ tsp) bicarbonate of soda
5g (1 tsp) cinnamon

For the cheesecake base

45g (¼ cup) plain flour
170g (1½ cups) cheesecake crumbs
150g (1 stick + 2½ tbsp) unsalted butter

For the cheesecake filling

1.3kg (2lb 14oz) Philadelphia cream cheese, or other full-fat soft cheese
315g (1½ cups + 1 tbsp) sugar
1 tsp vanilla extract
200g (¾ cup + 1 tbsp) double cream
125g egg (2 large eggs)
yolk from 2 large eggs
250g (1 cup + 1 tbsp) crème fraîche

For the cherry compote

900g (6½ cups) pitted cherries (fresh or frozen)
110g (½ cup + 1 tbsp) sugar
60g (¼ cup) sour cherry molasses

METHOD

Cheesecake crumb

1. Cream the sugars, honey, salt and butter using the paddle attachment so it is soft and fluffy. Mix the flour and bicarbonate of soda and cinnamon and add to the mix. Split the mixture into four and flatten it into a disc. Chill for half an hour in the fridge.

2. Roll the dough thinly and flat and place on a baking tray. Bake for 15 minutes at 170°C (150°C fan/340°F/gas mark 4). Once the mixture is cool, blitz it into crumbs.

Cheesecake base

Mix the flour and crumbs together. Melt the butter, then weigh precisely 130g (9 tablespoons) and pour onto the dry ingredients. Mix well. Flatten over the base of a 24cm (9in) round cake tin. Then bake for 7 minutes at 170°C (150°C fan/340°F/gas mark 4).

Fill and bake the cheesecake

1. Using a stand mixer fitted with the paddle attachment, beat the cream cheese, sugar and vanilla to a smooth and soft consistency. Add the cream and combine. Add the eggs gradually while mixing. Tip the mixture onto the base.

2. Bake in the oven at 90°C (70°C fan/190°F/gas mark ¼) for 2 hours and 5 minutes. Cool down and set in the fridge overnight. Then, using a pallet knife, smooth the crème fraîche on top.

Cherry compote

In a pan, bring the cherries and sugar to a boil. Reduce the heat and simmer for a further 2 minutes. Strain, setting aside the fruit for later, then keep reducing the water to a light syrup consistency. Add the cherry molasses and the strained cherries from earlier, then mix gently to combine. Leave to cool in the pan, then place the compote in an airtight container and store in the fridge for up to 24 hours.

To serve

Transfer the compote to a small serving dish and allow to come to room temperature. Spoon 1–2 tablespoons over each serving of cheesecake.

TOM KERRIDGE
Baked Vanilla Cheesecake

Baked cheesecakes have a rich and creamy texture and are more satisfying than their uncooked counterparts. Serve this classic baked vanilla cheesecake with ripe berries in the summer, or a spiced fruit compote in winter. It really is a pud for all seasons, so feel free to adapt it as you like.

SERVES 10

INGREDIENTS

For the base
225g (8oz) digestive biscuits or graham crackers
40g (3 tbsp + 1 tsp) sugar
100g (7 tbsp), butter, melted, plus extra for greasing

For the filling
750g (1lb 10oz) soft full-fat cream cheese, such as Philadelphia
400g (1¾ cups) crème fraîche
170g (¾ cup + 1 tbsp) sugar
45g (¼ cup) plain flour
pinch of salt
2 vanilla pods, split in half lengthways and seeds scraped out
finely grated zest and juice of 1 unwaxed lime
6 large egg yolks
seasonal fruit (optional)

METHOD

1. Preheat the oven to 180°C (160°C fan/350°F/gas mark 4). Lightly grease the base and sides of a 23cm (9in) round springform cake tin with butter and line with non-stick baking parchment. Butter the parchment.

2. To make the base, put the biscuits into a food processor and whiz to crumbs. Alternatively, place them in a self-sealing plastic bag and bash with a rolling pin until finely crushed. Tip the crumbs into a large bowl and stir in the sugar, add the melted butter and mix to combine.

3. Tip the crumb mixture into the prepared cake tin, spread evenly and press down firmly with the back of a spoon so the base is nice and compact. Bake for 10–15 minutes. Remove from the oven and leave to cool completely in the tin.

4. Meanwhile, prepare the filling. Using either a freestanding mixer fitted with the whisk attachment or an electric hand mixer and bowl, beat the cream cheese, crème fraîche and sugar together on a medium speed for a couple of minutes until the mixture is very smooth and creamy.

5. Sift the flour and salt over the mixture and mix again briefly, just to combine. Add the vanilla seeds, lime juice and zest, and whisk slowly, until evenly blended. Now incorporate the egg yolks one at a time, beating briefly after each addition and scraping the bowl down as necessary with a spatula. Do not overbeat – you want the filling to be smooth, light and aerated.

6. Pour the filling on top of the biscuit base, gently levelling out the surface with a spoon or a palette knife. Give the tin a gentle tap on a flat surface to ensure there are no air pockets in the mixture and stand the tin on a baking sheet.

7. Bake at 180°C (160°C fan/350°F/gas mark 4) for 10 minutes, then turn the oven down to 140°C (120°C fan/275°F/gas mark 1) and bake for a further 1 hour and 10 minutes. The filling should be set but have a slight wobble in the centre when you gently shake the tin. Do not overcook as it will firm up considerably as it cools.

8. Turn off the oven and prop the oven door open slightly. Leave the cheesecake inside to 'rest' for around 15–20 minutes, then remove from the oven and leave to stand at room temperature for at least 3 hours. It's now ready to serve but can be chilled if you're not eating it straight. To unmould the cheesecake, run a knife around the edge of the tin, removing the parchment, and transfer the cheesecake to a plate, cut into wedges and serve just as it is, or with fruit.

SIVAN KOBI
Lotus Biscoff No-Bake Cheesecake

This recipe was one of my first and it is still my most-asked-about cake! It can be enjoyed for up to a week refrigerated (if it lasts).

SERVES 8–10

INGREDIENTS

For the crust
1 full pack (250g/9oz) Biscoff biscuits
120g (¾ cup) chocolate chips, melted
115g (1 stick) unsalted butter, melted

For the filling
225g (8oz) cream cheese
235g (1 cup) sour cream
470ml (2 cups) whipping cream
40g (⅓ cup) icing sugar

For the topping
About 10 Biscoff biscuits, crumbled, for crumbing the outside of the cake (optional)
240ml (1 cup) Lotus cookie butter, melted
whipped cream dollops made from 120ml (½ cup) whipping cream whisked with 1 tbsp icing sugar
additional crumbs to go on top of the dollops (optional)

METHOD

Cheesecake crust

1. Crumb the biscuits in a food processor or a handy manual chopper. Then melt the chocolate and butter in a microwave separately.

2. Have ready a 23cm (9in) springform cake tin. Place the crumbs in a bowl and pour over the chocolate and butter. Mix until combined and place into the ungreased tin. No need to spray the tin. Using the back of a spoon, press in the crumbs, packing them nicely.

Filling and topping

1. Using a stand or hand mixer with the whip attachment, place all of your ingredients for the filling into the bowl. Whip till completely whipped and sturdy – about 5–7 minutes on medium to high. Spread the filling on top of the base and smooth it out. Cover with clingfilm and refrigerate for a few hours or overnight.

2. Slide a knife around the edge of the tin then release the outer ring and remove the cake, still on its base. If desired, crumb the extra biscuits and press them against the sides of the cake. Melt the cookie butter in the microwave for just 30 seconds. Pour over the top of your cake and smooth it out to the edge of the crumbs. Alternatively, instead of adding crumbs to the sides of the cake, allow the melted cookie butter to drip along the sides of the cake.

3. If having dollops on top, whip together the cream and sugar until it holds soft peaks. Place in a piping bag with a medium open star tip (I use a Wilton 1M tip). Pipe dollops on top of the cake and sprinkle with lotus crumbs. Enjoy!

LEAH KOENIG
Ricotta Cheesecake (Cassola)

This ricotta cheesecake was likely introduced to Rome by Sephardi Jews who fled Sicily during the Spanish Inquisition. The dish was originally cooked in a pan set on the stovetop, like a frittata or oversized pancake. Over time, a baked version (also called channà) emerged and became a favourite of both Jewish and non-Jewish Romans. Today, baked cassola is a popular Christmas dessert amongst the city's Catholic community. Roman Jews, meanwhile, enjoy it on Shavuot, when dairy dishes are commonly served. On a visit to Rome, I enjoyed a memorably light and delicately sweet wedge of cassola at the kosher restaurant Yotvata, located just beyond the Jewish Ghetto neighbourhood. My version is inspired by that tasty memory.

SERVES 6–8

INGREDIENTS

unsalted butter and unseasoned breadcrumbs, for the cake tin
720g (3 cups) whole milk ricotta, drained through a sieve for 30 minutes
150g (¾ cup) sugar
3 large eggs
1 tbsp cornflour or potato starch
1½ tsp vanilla extract
1 tsp ground cinnamon
¼ tsp kosher salt or fine sea salt
45g (⅓ cup) raisins or sultanas (optional)
icing sugar, for dusting

METHOD

1. Preheat the oven to 180°C (160°C fan/350°F/gas mark 4) and generously grease a 20cm (8in) round, tall-sided cake tin with butter. Add a small handful of breadcrumbs to the tin and tilt it in all directions to lightly coat the bottom and sides. Pour out and discard the excess breadcrumbs and set the tin aside.

2. Add the ricotta, sugar, eggs, cornflour, vanilla, cinnamon and salt to the bowl of a stand mixer fitted with a paddle blade (or use a large bowl and an electric hand mixer). Beat at medium speed until fully combined and smooth (there will still be some texture from the ricotta), about 1 minute. Stir in the raisins, if using.

3. Transfer the mixture to the prepared cake tin and bake until puffed and golden on top and set at the centre with just a hint of jiggle, 50 to 60 minutes.

4. Place the cake tin on a wire rack to cool completely. (Do not cut the cassola while it is still hot.) When cool, use a fine mesh sieve to dust the top with confectioner's sugar and serve at room temperature. Store leftovers, covered, in the fridge for up to three days.

PIERRE KOFFMANN
Vanilla Cheesecake with Red Berry Compote

A slice of this dreamy vanilla cheesecake will not be enough, so it's a good job this baked cheesecake recipe produces a whole cake for you to devour in your own time. A mixed berry compote cuts through the richness of the cake perfectly. This recipe first appeared on the Great British Chefs website.

INGREDIENTS

For the cheesecake mix
880g (1lb 15oz) cream cheese
210g (1 cup + 1 tbsp) sugar
4 vanilla pods, de-seeded
2 egg yolks
2 eggs
250ml (1 cup) double cream

For the crumble mix
70g (½ cup) demerara sugar
70g (½ cup) plain flour
70g (½ cup) ground hazelnuts
70g (5 tbsp) butter

For the cake base and topping
55g (4 tbsp) butter, melted
300g (1¼ cups) crème fraîche

For the mixed berry compote
350g (1¾ cups) demerara sugar
750ml (3 cups + 2 tbsp) red wine
1 cinnamon stick
1 star anise
250g (2 cups) raspberries
250g (2 cups) fresh blackberries
250g (1⅓ cups) blueberries

To finish
1 vanilla pod, dried

METHOD

1. Preheat the oven to 110°C (90°C fan/230°F/gas mark ¼).

2. Begin by preparing the cheesecake mix. Combine the cream cheese, sugar and vanilla in a mixer and mix on a medium speed until combined. Add the eggs, continue to mix on a medium speed, then switch to a low speed and add the cream, allowing it to combine slowly. Turn up to a high speed and mix for 1 minute until thickened.

3. Place a 22cm (9in) deep square cake tin, or a 23cm (9in) round springform cake tin if you'd like a circular cheesecake, onto a flat baking tray. Butter the cake tin. Fill the tin with the cheesecake mixture until it is just below the top of the tin.

4. Bake the cheesecake in the oven for 55 minutes until the top is just firm to gentle touch, baking for an additional 5–10 minutes if necessary. Remove from the oven and allow to cool to room temperature – it should still wobble slightly. Once cool, place in the fridge to set. for 4–6 hours, or overnight.

5. Preheat the oven to 160°C (140°C fan/320°F/gas mark 3). Now, make the crumble mix. Combine all the dry ingredients in a bowl, then dice the butter and rub into the dry ingredients. Once all the butter is incorporated, spread out on a baking tray lined with baking paper. Bake the crumble in the oven for 25 minutes, or until golden brown and crunchy. Remove from the oven and set aside to cool.

6. To prepare the base, break the crumble into little pieces and then blitz in a food processor with the melted butter. Spread this mixture evenly across the baking paper-lined base of a 24cm (9in) square or 23cm (9in) round springform cake tin. Refrigerate until set.

7. To assemble, remove the cheesecake and base from the fridge. Loosen the springform tin around the base, and lift it off so you're left with just the base. Place the crumble base on top of the chilled cheesecake, crumble side down, and place a tray on top. Invert so that the base is on the bottom. Mix the crème fraîche in a bowl until it becomes runny, then spread evenly over the top of the cheesecake, ensuring that it only just reaches the top of the tin. Refrigerate to set for at least an hour.

8. To prepare the berry compote, add the sugar, red wine, cinnamon stick and star anise to a medium-sized pan and bring to the boil. Reduce by half, then reduce the temperature to a simmer. Add the fruit and simmer until soft and tender. Remove the fruit from the poaching liquid and reduce the liquid by half over a high heat. Once reduced, pour the remaining liquid back over the fruit and set aside until ready to plate.

9. Remove the cheesecake from the fridge. Carefully slide off the ring section of the tin, maintaining the form and shape of the cheesecake. To plate, dip your knife in hot water and then wipe it on a clean tea towel before using it to slice the cheesecake into portions. Garnish with the mixed berry compote and a slither of dried vanilla pod.

KIM KUSHNER
Cheesecake, Israeli-Style

Israeli cheesecake is totally different from American cheesecake. It is creamy and cool and sandwiched between a biscuit-like, buttery, flaky crust and crumbs. It's quite simple to prepare and requires minimal baking (just the crust and crumbs are baked), unlike many cheesecakes that require complex baking techniques. Believe me, you want to make this cake and you'll be glad that you did.

SERVES 8–10

INGREDIENTS

For the crust and crumbs

190g (1½ cups) all-purpose flour
1 tsp baking powder
¼ tsp salt
115g (1 stick) butter, cubed
100g (½ cup) sugar
1 tsp vanilla extract
3 egg yolks

For the cheesecake filling

510g (2 cups) double cream
200g (1 cup) sugar
1 tsp vanilla extract or seeds from 1 vanilla pod
680g (3 x 8oz packs) cream cheese, softened
zest of 1 lemon

METHOD

1. Preheat the oven to 180°C (160°C fan/350°F/gas mark 4) and line two 23cm (9in) springform cake tins with parchment paper.

2. In a medium-sized bowl, stir together the flour, baking powder and salt. Set aside. Using a hand mixer or a stand mixer fitted with the paddle attachment, combine the butter and sugar. Mix on medium-high for 2 minutes, until creamy. Add the vanilla and eggs. Mix on medium speed until combined, about 1 minute. Then add the flour mixture and stir on medium speed until a dough is formed.

3. Divide the dough into two equal-sized balls. Use your fingertips to press one dough ball into one of the cake tins in an even layer. Repeat with the remaining dough ball in the second tin. Bake for 20 minutes, until golden. Remove the two cake tins from the oven and set aside to cool completely.

4. Meanwhile, prepare the cheesecake filling. Using a hand mixer or a stand mixer fitted with the whisk attachment, combine the cream, sugar and vanilla and beat until stiff peaks form, about 5 minutes. Switch to the paddle attachment. Add the cream cheese and lemon zest to the bowl. Mix on medium speed until all is well combined.

5. Pour the cheesecake filling over the crust that is in one of the cake tins. Use a spatula to spread it into an even layer. Use your hands to crumble the remaining crust into fine crumbs. Sprinkle the crumbs all over the top of the cheese filling. Cover with clingfilm and refrigerate for 4 hours or overnight. Before serving, carefully remove from the tin, peel away the parchment paper and transfer to a serving plate.

COOK'S TIPS
- To line a springform cake tin with parchment paper, trace the tin on a large piece of parchment paper with a pen or a pencil. Use scissors to cut out the traced shape. Spray the tin lightly with cooking oil and press the parchment paper into the base of the tin.
- The crust and crumbs can be prepared up to 1 month in advance and wrapped tightly in clingfilm and kept in the freezer until ready to assemble. Alternatively, they can be prepared up to three days in advance and wrapped tightly in clingfilm and kept in a cool, dry place until ready to assemble. The cheese filling can be prepared up to 2 hours in advance before assembling.

MARIE LAFORÊT
Pink Velvet Cheesecake

SERVES 8

INGREDIENTS

For the biscuit base
200g (1⅔ cups) vegan chocolate biscuits, crushed
3 tbsp melted coconut oil

For the filling
125g (¾ cup) hulled strawberries
125g (¾ cup) raspberries
4 tbsp oat cream
1 uncooked beetroot, roughly chopped
400g (1½ cups) firm tofu, roughly chopped
150g (⅔ cup) silken tofu
90g (¼ cup + 3 tbsp) light brown sugar
6 tbsp cashew butter
6 tbsp cornflour

For the jellied coulis
250g (1¼ cups) hulled strawberries
100ml (¼ cup + 3 tbsp) water
½ tsp agar-agar powder
3 tbsp light brown sugar

METHOD
Biscuit base
Use a fork to combine the crushed biscuits with the coconut oil. Spread evenly in a springform tin about 25cm (10in) in diameter and use a flat-bottomed tumbler to press down well. Refrigerate for 15 minutes.

Cheesecake filling
1. Whiz the strawberries and raspberries with the oat cream, then strain through a sieve to remove the seeds. Whiz the beetroot with a little water to obtain its juice. Set 8 tablespoons of it aside.

2. Whiz all the remaining filling ingredients together, then combine with the berry and oat cream mix and the beetroot juice. Pour onto the biscuit base and bake for about 45 minutes at 180°C (160°C fan/350°F/gas mark 4). The top of the cheesecake should be firm. Leave to cool to room temperature.

Jellied coulis
1. Whiz the strawberries and the water, then strain through a sieve to remove the seeds. Pour into a small saucepan and add the agar-agar and sugar. Mix well. Bring to the boil and stir for 2 minutes. Pour over the cheesecake.

2. Leave to cool and refrigerate for 2 hours. Carefully unmould just before serving. Keeps well for two days in the fridge.

COOK'S TIP
- Make this cheesecake the day before to save work on the 'big day'.

DAVID LEBOVITZ
Cheesecake Brownies

INGREDIENTS

For the brownies

85g (6 tbsp) unsalted butter, cut into pieces
115g (4oz) bittersweet or semisweet chocolate, chopped
130g (⅔ cup) sugar
2 large eggs, at room temperature
70g (½ cup) all-purpose flour
1 tbsp unsweetened cocoa powder, natural or Dutch process
⅛ tsp salt
1 tsp vanilla extract
80g (½ cup) chocolate chips

For the cheesecake topping

225g (9oz) cream cheese, at room temperature
1 large egg yolk
75g (generous ⅓ cup) sugar
⅛ tsp vanilla extract

METHOD

1. Preheat the oven to 180°C (160°C fan/350°F/gas mark 4) and line a 23cm (9in) or 20cm (8in) square cake tin with foil, making sure it goes up all four sides. Use two sheets if necessary. Mist with non-stick spray or grease lightly.

2. To make the brownie batter, melt the butter and chocolate in a medium saucepan over a low heat, stirring until smooth. Remove from the heat and beat in the sugar, then the eggs. Mix in the flour, cocoa powder and salt, then the vanilla and chocolate chips. Spread evenly in the prepared cake tin.

3. For the cheesecake topping, in a separate bowl, beat together the cream cheese, egg yolk, sugar and vanilla until smooth. Distribute the cream cheese mixture in eight dollops across the top of the brownie mixture, then take a dull knife or spatula and swirl the cream cheese mixture with the chocolate batter. Rap the cake tin on a countertop a few times to let the batter and swirl settle together.

4. Bake until the batter in the centre of the cake tin feels just set, 35 to 40 minutes. Let cool, then lift the brownies out holding the foil and peel it away. Cut the brownies into squares.

COOK'S TIP

- These cheesecake brownies will keep in an airtight container for a couple of days. They also freeze well for up to two months. I recommend freezing them individually so you can remove them one at a time.

SHARON LURIE
Bobba's Cheesecake with Caramel Apples and Streusel Topping

Everybody has their 'best cheesecake recipe ever'. Whether you're adding a couple of extras such as apples, strawberries or chocolate to a basic recipe, the basic ingredients have to be there. After experimenting with cheesecake recipes for many years, I still hold onto my mother's basic recipe as 'The Best', and to that I've added a couple of twists here and there for a decadent look and taste. Here's her basic recipe with the addition of apples and a streusel topping, or if you're in the mood for something really decadent, try the optional decorative topping.

SERVES 8

INGREDIENTS

For the base
1 box Nuttikrust biscuits or 200g (7oz) of your favourite tea biscuits
150g (1 stick + 3 tbsp) butter, melted

For the filling
3 extra large eggs
150g (¾ cup) sugar
3 x 250g tubs (1lb 10z) full-fat cream cheese
125ml (½ cup) sour cream
40g (⅓ cup) plain flour
1 tsp vanilla extract
1 tsp lemon juice
1 x 495g can (4 cups) pie apples
2 tsp ground cinnamon
3 tbsp brown sugar

For the streusel topping
200g (1 cup) soft brown sugar
80g (½ cup) plain flour
pinch of salt
3 tbsp butter
1 tbsp ground cinnamon

METHOD

1. Crush the biscuits in a food processor (or with a rolling pin), then mix with the melted butter until smooth. Line the base of a springform cake tin with the mixture and refrigerate while preparing the filling and topping.

2. In the bowl of a food processor or stand mixer, beat the eggs and sugar together until light and creamy. Reduce the speed and slowly add cream cheese, sour cream, flour, vanilla extract and lemon juice until well blended. Do not overbeat as it may cause the top to crack. Pour half of the mixture over the cold biscuit base. Delicately place the pie apples over the cream cheese mixture and sprinkle with the cinnamon and brown sugar. Cover the apples with the remaining cream cheese mixture.

3. Preheat the oven to 180°C (160°C fan/350°F/gas mark 4). Combine the streusel topping ingredients, then crumble the mixture with the tips of your fingers. Sprinkle the mixture over the top of the unbaked cheesecake.

4. Bake, uncovered, for 20 minutes, then reduce the temperature to 160°C (140°C fan/325°F/gas mark 3) and bake for another 15 minutes. Switch the oven off and leave the cheesecake inside for a further 15 minutes. If necessary, place a sheet of aluminium foil on the cheesecake after the first 20 minutes – if the streusel is golden-brown already – but continue to bake at the lower heat as the cheesecake still has to cook through the middle.

For the decorative topping (optional)*
1 large Granny Smith apple, peeled, cored and very thinly sliced
1 tbsp butter
2 tbsp syrup
3 tbsp fresh cream

5. Remove from the oven and allow the cake to cool completely in the tin. Before removing from the tin, run a knife between the outer edge of the cake and the inside of the tin. Position the cake on a serving dish and carefully release the spring.

*If you're opting for something more decadent, fry the Granny Smith apple in the butter and syrup until soft and the liquid has turned to caramel. Just before serving the cake, pour the mixture over the top.

SARAH MANN-YEAGER
Grandma Anne's Perfectly Retro Baked Cheesecake

Studded with sultanas and a delicious lemony sharpness that cuts through the richness, this deeply decadent cheesecake is one of those dishes that takes me straight back to my childhood. I prefer to make mine in a deep 20cm (8in) springform tin with a height of just under 9cm (3½in). If you only have a shallow 22cm–23cm (9in) springform tin, use the smaller quantities given for the filling ingredients.

SERVES 12–16

INGREDIENTS

For the pastry base
200g (1¾ sticks) soft unsalted butter
100g (½ cup) sugar
300g (scant 2½ cups) plain flour
1 large egg beaten

For the filling
750g–1kg (3–4 cups) curd cheese or medium fat soft cheese
150g–200g (¾–1 cup) sugar
75g–100g (⅓–½ cup) sour cream
zest of ½–1 lemon
75g–100g (½–⅔ cup) sultanas (optional)
2–3 medium eggs
2–3 medium egg yolks
1 tsp vanilla extract (optional)
50–75g (scant ½ cup, plus more as needed) plain flour
mixed berries and/or fruit coulis, to serve

METHOD

1. Lightly grease and line your regular or deep springform cake tin. Beat the butter and sugar together with a hand or stand mixer until light and fluffy. Add the flour and mix to combine. Remove half the dough from the bowl and press into the bottom of the cake tin.

2. Add half the beaten egg to the rest of the pastry and mix well to combine. Shape the remaining pastry into a disc, wrap in clingfilm and refrigerate along with the pastry-lined tin for one hour.

3. Preheat the oven to 180°C (160°C fan/350°F/gas mark 4).

4. Prick the pastry in the tin with a fork, and blind bake for approximately 15 minutes by covering with parchment and weighting it down with baking beans. Remove the baking beans and parchment and return to the oven for approximately 5 minutes until the pastry is pale gold in colour. Remove and allow to cool in the tin.

5. Take the remaining pastry out of the fridge, roll it out between two sheets of non-stick baking parchment to a thickness of approximately 2.5mm (⅛in) and then cut into long strips about 1cm (½in) wide. Place the strips on a parchment-lined baking sheet and put back into the fridge.

6. For the filling, combine the curd cheese and half the sugar in a large mixing bowl; add the sour cream, lemon zest, sultanas (optional) and mix well. Beat the eggs and egg yolks with the remaining sugar and vanilla extract, if using, and then fold this into the cheese mixture. Fold in the flour. Scrape the mixture into the pastry-lined tin, level the surface by gently banging the tin on your worktop a couple of times and then even with a spatula.

7. Now arrange the pastry strips in a lattice pattern over the top. Brush with the reserved beaten egg and bake on the middle shelf for approximately 60–70 minutes until the top is browned and the cheesecake is set but still retains a little wobble in the centre. Check the cake after 40 minutes and again after 50 minutes: if it is browning too quickly, cover the top loosely with a sheet of parchment paper.

8. Allow the cake to cool in the tin before removing to a serving plate. Top with fresh berries of your choice and a little fruit coulis if desired.

COOK'S TIPS

- Cut the parchment for the base of the tin about 8–10cm (3–4in) bigger than your tin and allow it to hang outside the tin. Then cut a circle of parchment to fit the tin and place inside. When you come to remove the cake, sit the tin on a can of baked beans, or something similar, and allow the unclipped ring to drop down; you can then grab the edges of the parchment and slide the cake onto your serving plate.
- It is better to mix the filling ingredients by hand as you will want the texture to be quite dense and using a mixer will add too many air bubbles. If you can't manage, use the paddle rather than the balloon whisk attachment and do it in short bursts.
- This cheesecake can sometimes sink in the middle; to stop this from happening, turn the oven off then half open the oven door and allow the cake to cool for about 40 minutes. This will also help prevent cracking.

GILL MELLER
Blackcurrant, Thyme and Goat's Cheesecake

Soft, creamy goat's cheese is delicate in flavour and adds the perfect balance of savouriness. Gill Meller pairs it with an oaty base and sweet-tart blackcurrants in this easy, no-bake cheesecake from *delicious*.

SERVES 6 with leftovers

INGREDIENTS

For the base
150g (5oz) digestive biscuits or graham crackers
125g (1 stick + 1 tbsp) unsalted butter
1 tbsp clear honey
50g (½ cup) jumbo or old-fashioned rolled oats, toasted in a dry pan
finely grated zest of 1 orange

For the filling
1 vanilla pod
300ml (1¼ cup) double cream
65g (⅓ cup) sugar
250g (1¾ cup) fresh soft goat's cheese

For the topping
1½ gelatine leaves (we used Costa)
200g (2 cups) blackcurrants, washed and stalks removed
50g (¼ cup) sugar
3–4 fresh thyme sprigs

METHOD

1. For the base, put the biscuits in a food processor, whizz to fine crumbs, then set aside. Melt the butter and honey in a saucepan, then add the crushed digestive biscuits, toasted oats and orange zest. Mix well. Press the mixture into the base of a 20cm (8in) loose-bottomed tart tin and chill for 1 hour to set.

2. Meanwhile, split the vanilla pod and scrape the seeds into a mixing bowl. Add the cream and sugar, then whisk using an electric mixer until the cream forms stiff peaks when the beaters are removed.

3. Crumble the goat's cheese into the bowl, gently folding it into the cream until thoroughly combined. Spread the mix over the set biscuit base and return to the fridge to set for 1 hour.

4. Meanwhile for the topping, soak the gelatine leaves in cold water for 5 minutes to soften. Put the blackcurrants in a saucepan with 1 teaspoon of water, the sugar and the thyme. Cook gently, stirring often, until the berries are soft but still hold most of their shape, about 5 minutes. Squeeze the water from the gelatine leaves, then stir gently into the berries. Leave the mixture to cool to room temperature.

5. Remove the thyme sprigs from the cooled blackcurrant topping, then spoon it over the creamy goat's cheese layer (you might not need all the juice if there's a lot). Chill one last time for at least 3–4 hours or until the topping has set completely. Remove from the tin and serve.

THOMASINA MIERS
Vanilla Cheesecake with Pineapple Caramel

This is no ordinary cheesecake. The Mexican cheesecake is light, fluffy and volcanic-looking, cracked across the top to reveal an irresistibly delicate middle. A delicious pudding, with or without the wicked pineapple caramel.

SERVES 8–10

INGREDIENTS

40g (3 tbsp) butter
140g (5oz) Hobnob biscuits or other oat biscuits
225g (1 cup + 2 tbsp) sugar
2 tbsp cornflour
750g (1lb 10oz) cream cheese
6 large eggs, separated
½ tsp vanilla extract
150ml (½ cup + 1 tbsp) double cream
150ml (⅔ cup) sour cream
pinch of sea salt
zest of 1 lime

For the caramel
large knob of butter
200g (1 cup) fresh pineapple, peeled, cored and chopped into small pieces
pinch of sea salt
225g (1 cup + 2 tbsp) sugar
240ml (1 cup) water
handful of fresh raspberries, to serve (optional)

METHOD

1. Preheat the oven to 150°C (120°C fan/300°F/gas mark 2). Lightly grease a 26cm (10in) springform cake tin and line the base and sides with baking paper.

2. To make the base, melt the butter and whiz the biscuits in a food processor. Mix together and gently flatten on to the base of the tin. Put it in the fridge to chill. Meanwhile, mix the sugar and cornflour together. Beat in the cream cheese, egg yolks and vanilla extract with an electric whisk. Gradually add the creams, whisking as you do so. Finally add the salt and lime zest.

3. In a separate bowl, whisk the egg whites to stiff peaks, then fold them carefully into the cheese mixture with a large metal spoon (you want to keep all the air and lightness in the cake). Pour on to the chilled base and bake in the oven for 1 hour 15 minutes, or until the cheesecake is golden on top, trying not to open the oven door! Turn off the oven and leave the cheesecake to completely cool in the oven and only then remove the baking paper.

4. For the caramel, first melt the butter in a hot pan and fry the pineapple until it is caramelised and golden, seasoning it with the salt and 1 teaspoon of the sugar. Remove from the pan and add the rest of the sugar together with 120ml (½ cup) water. When the sugar has dissolved, turn the heat right up until the sugar has turned a deep, dark golden colour.

5. Turn the heat down, add another 120ml (½ cup) water, watching for the caramel's spitting, and let it bubble for a few minutes so that the sugar dissolves again and the syrup thickens. Add the pineapple and serve drizzled over the cheesecake or, if it is summer, have the cheesecake with heaps of raspberries.

HANNAH MILES
White Chocolate and Pistachio Cheesecake

This vibrant green pistachio cheesecake is sweetened with white chocolate and nestled in a bitter chocolate base. The best type of pistachio nuts to use are pistachio nibs, which are bright green – often found in Turkish and Iranian supermarkets. I always stock up when I find them as they make any dessert look pretty.

SERVES 12

INGREDIENTS

For the base
250g (9oz) Oreo cookies or chocolate biscuits
125g (1 stick) butter, melted

For the pistachio paste
200g (1½ cups) pistachio nuts
1 tbsp icing sugar
1–2 tbsp flavourless oil, such as vegetable or sunflower oil

For the cheesecake
3 sheets leaf gelatine (platinum grade)
300g (1½ cups) mascarpone cheese
250ml (1 cup) double cream
150g (5¼oz) white chocolate, chopped

METHOD

1. For the base, crush the Oreo cookies to fine crumbs in a food processor or blender, or place the cookies in a clean plastic bag and bash with a rolling pin. In a bowl, stir the melted butter into the crumbs and then press into the base of the tin tightly with the back of a spoon.

2. Reserve a small handful of pistachio nuts for decoration and place the rest with the icing sugar in a food processor or blender with 1 tbsp of the oil. Blitz until the nuts are very fine and you have a thick paste. If the mixture is too dry, add a little more oil and blitz again.

3. For the cheesecake, soak the gelatine leaves in water until they are soft. Whisk the mascarpone cheese and pistachio nut paste together until light and creamy.

4. Place the cream in a pan and warm gently. Squeeze the water out of the gelatine leaves and stir into the warm cream (removed from the heat) until the gelatine has dissolved. Pass this mixture through a sieve or strainer to remove any undissolved gelatine, then add 100g (3¼oz) of the chopped white chocolate to the warm cream and whisk until melted.

5. Pour the cream into the pistachio mixture and whisk together. Pour the filling on to the base. Finely chop the reserved pistachio nuts and sprinkle over the top of the cheesecake with the remaining chopped white chocolate.

6. Leave to set in the refrigerator for 3 hours or overnight before serving. The cheesecake will keep in the refrigerator for up to 3 days.

MONDAY MORNING COOKING CLUB
South African Cheesecake

This type of biscuit-based, baked cheesecake is a staple in Sydney's Jewish community at Shavuot, introduced by the many wonderful cooks from South Africa who now call Australia home. This one is from our friend Dorryce Rock who is well known for this super creamy, light and irresistible cheesecake. It is now one of the Monday Morning Cooking Club's most popular recipes.

SERVES about 12

INGREDIENTS

375g (13oz) plain sweet biscuits, such as Marie or digestive biscuits or graham crackers
pinch of salt
250g (2 sticks + 2 tbsp) unsalted butter, melted
8 eggs, separated
230g (1 cup) sugar
750g (1lb 10oz) cream cheese, at room temperature, chopped
150ml (scant ⅔ cup) whipping cream

METHOD

1. Preheat the oven to 180°C (160°C fan/350°F/gas mark 4). You will need a deep 3 litre (12 cup) baking dish. To make the cheesecake base, put the biscuits and salt in a food processor and process until they resemble breadcrumbs. Add the butter and pulse to combine. Tip the mixture into the base of the baking dish and press it evenly into the base and up the sides.

2. Using an electric mixer, beat the egg yolks until light and fluffy, adding the sugar gradually. Add the cream cheese one third at a time and beat on high speed to ensure there are no lumps. On medium speed, slowly add the cream and beat until smooth.

3. In a separate bowl, whisk the egg whites just until stiff peaks form. Using a spatula or metal spoon, gently fold the egg whites into the cream cheese mixture, one third at a time, then pour the mixture into the prepared crust. Bake for 45 minutes or until golden brown on top (probably with cracks) but still quite wobbly.

4. Turn the oven off and leave the cheesecake to set in the oven for 10 minutes. Serve at room temperature. To serve, scoop with a large spoon straight from the baking dish to a plate. Refrigerate any leftovers.

NOTE:
This cake can also be made in a lined 26cm (10½in) springform tin. When completely cool, remove from the tin and slice to serve.

YANIR MREJEN
Shavuot Cheesecake Made Easy

We wanted to share a delicious recipe from Chef Yanir Mrejen for an easy, creamy cheesecake recipe that's traditionally enjoyed on the holiday of Shavuot. Shavuot, which celebrates God's giving of the Torah to the Jewish people on Mount Sinai, is also known as a 'dairy' holiday where cheesecake is a big feature.

INGREDIENTS

For the base
75g (5 tbsp) unsalted butter
150g (1 rounded cup) plain flour
50g (scant ½ cup) icing sugar
  pinch of salt
1 egg yolk

For the filling
500ml (2 cups) double cream
1 tsp vanilla syrup
120g (1 cup) icing sugar, split into
  two equal portions
zest of 1 lemon
500g (1lb 1½oz) low-fat cream
  cheese
400g (14oz) full-fat cream cheese

METHOD

1. Place a piece of parchment paper over the bottom of a 30cm (12in) springform tin, then seal the tin edge around the base. Grease the inner sides of the tin with butter or cooking spray.

2. In a bowl, rub together the butter and flour with your fingertips until it resembles breadcrumbs. Mix in the icing sugar with a pinch of salt, then the egg yolk. If the pastry feels too dry to form a dough, add 1 tablespoon of water.

3. Shape the dough into a ball and flatten out into a disc, then wrap in clingfilm to chill in the fridge for at least 30 minutes before using. During this time, preheat the oven to 170°C (150°C fan/340°F/gas mark 4).

4. Bake the base until golden brown (around 20 minutes). Leave to cool slightly as you make the filling. Once the base is out of the oven, make the filling by mixing together the cream, vanilla syrup, half of the icing sugar and the lemon zest.

5. In a separate bowl, whisk together the cream cheeses and the other half of the icing sugar. With a large spoon, combine the two mixtures together until it forms a smooth and creamy filling.

6. Fill the now cooled pastry (or biscuit) base with the creamy cheesecake filling and leave in the fridge to set overnight. Once set, you can add any topping you like, from fresh fruit and compote topping to biscuits crumbs or chocolate syrup... Enjoy!

COOK'S TIP
- If strapped for time, an easier way to make this base is to use 250g (2 cups) of your favourite digestive biscuits and combine with 100g (7 tablespoons) of melted butter. Mix together to form an even mixture and lightly press down in the cake tin to form the base. Bake until golden brown.

SILVIA NACAMULLI
Amaretto and Raspberry Cheesecake

Cheesecake has only become popular in Italy over the last few decades, so this is a new-generation recipe. As a newcomer, there is no Italian word for it, so the English 'cheesecake' has been adopted. A few years back, I created this no-bake recipe for Shavuot, when Jews traditionally eat dairy, hence have cheesy desserts of all kinds!

I wanted to combine this tradition with the novelty of using Italian ingredients, such as Amaretti biscuits and mascarpone cheese. It quickly became a family favourite, and a classic for Shavuot and the summer months that follow. The flavours are rich and fresh at the same time. I really like the raspberries on top, but you can replace them with mixed fresh berries or conserve, if you prefer, or use both!

SERVES 6–8

INGREDIENTS

80g (3oz) Amaretti biscuits
80g (3oz) digestive biscuits or graham crackers
80g (6 tbsp) soft butter
250g (1 cup) mascarpone cheese
200g (7oz) cream cheese
80g (⅔ cup) icing sugar
grated zest of 1 lemon
1 tsp vanilla extract
pinch of sea salt
100ml (¼ cup + 3 tbsp) whipping or double cream
200–250g (1¾–2 cups) raspberries
mint leaves and icing sugar to decorate

METHOD

1. Line a 20cm (8in) springform oven tin with baking parchment.

2. Crumble the biscuits in a food processor. Add the butter and blitz until the mixture clumps together. Press the biscuit mixture evenly in a single layer into the tin and put it in the fridge while preparing the cheese mixture.

3. Whisk the mascarpone, cream cheese, icing sugar, zest, vanilla extract and salt. Lightly whip the double cream and fold it into the cheese mixture. Pour the filling onto the biscuit base and spread it evenly with a spatula.

4. Cover with clingfilm and refrigerate for a minimum of 4 hours before serving. Just before serving, scatter plenty of raspberries over the top of the cake and scatter over a few mint leaves. Sift over a little icing sugar. Serve chilled.

SILVIA NACAMULLI
Tiramisù

Does tiramisu count as a cheesecake? It's debatable but since it is one of my signature dishes (and one of my publisher's favourites), and it uses a whole tub of mascarpone cheese it seems reasonable to include! There is no alcohol in my recipe, however, should you prefer it with alcohol, then add 2–3 tablespoons of Marsala, rum or sherry (or other alcohol of your choice) to the coffee before dipping the biscuits in (and/or add it to the mascarpone mixture). Good-quality ingredients are key here, so I recommend using Italian *savoiardi*, mascarpone cheese and espresso coffee, and make sure the eggs are very fresh as otherwise it won't hold firm and the cheese mixture becomes runny.

SERVES 6–8

INGREDIENTS

about 500ml (17fl oz/ generous 2 cups) espresso coffee or strong black coffee
2–3 tablespoons milk
5 large eggs
5 tablespoons caster or granulated sugar
pinch of sea salt
500g (2 cups) mascarpone cheese
about 300g (10oz) *savoiardi* biscuits (ladies' fingers or sponge fingers)
cocoa powder, to dust

COOK'S TIPS

- Don't soak the *savoiardi* for too long, as they need to be soft on the outside but still a little dry inside.
- This lasts up to 3 days, covered, in the fridge, and its flavour changes slightly with time, as the *savoiardi* absorb more of the coffee and cheese cream.

METHOD

1. First, make the coffee so it has time to cool down a little. Once it's ready, pour it into a shallow bowl and add the milk – the milk softens its flavour and reduces the temperature.

2. Separate the eggs. Beat the yolks with 3 tablespoons of the sugar (keeping 2 tablespoons aside to whisk with the egg whites later) for a couple of minutes until pale and creamy, either in a bowl with an electric hand mixer or in the bowl of a stand mixer fitted with the paddle attachment. Add the salt and stir.

3. Add the mascarpone cheese, a tablespoon at a time, gently whisking it in (either by hand this time, or using the lowest speed setting of the hand or stand mixer) until just combined.

4. In a separate, clean bowl, whisk the egg whites with an electric hand mixer (attachments cleaned and dried if you used them for the egg yolks, sugar and mascarpone) for about 1 minute until they form soft peaks, then add the 2 tablespoons of sugar you set aside earlier, continuing to whisk for at least 1 minute at high speed until the whites form stiff peaks. Slowly fold them into the mascarpone and egg yolk mixture with a metal spoon or spatula – adding the sugar to the whisked egg whites helps hold the mixture together.

5. Spread a thin coat of the mascarpone mixture on the base of a square, oval or round dish about 30 x 25cm (12 x 10in). Dip the *savoiardi* on both sides into the coffee, one at a time, and place them close together over the mascarpone mixture until you have a single layer.

6. Spread half of the remaining mascarpone mixture uniformly over the biscuits. Cover it with a second layer of *savoiardi* dipped in coffee, then spread the remaining mascarpone mixture on top. Keep chilled for at least 2 hours until ready to serve. If it's going to be in the fridge for more than 2–3 hours, then cover it with clingfilm.

7. Sift cocoa powder over the top and serve chilled, always.

JOAN NATHAN
Roman Ricotta Cheese Crostata with Cherries or Chocolate

When in Rome, do as the Romans do: head straight to the tiny nondescript Pasticceria Boccione (also known as the Burnt Bakery or the Jewish bakery) in the *ghetto ebraico* (Jewish Ghetto) near the Tiber. There, four sisters make the same slightly burnt baked goods until they run out each day. Whether composed of tourists or locals, there is always a line outside. One of the popular staples is a rich ricotta cake wrapped in a crostata crust, called cassola, a Christmas must in Rome. According to Clifford Wright, the Jews of Rome learnt to make whey cheese in Sicily and brought the technique with them to Rome. I have added a delicious Italian crostata that I learnt from an Italian Jew in place of the heavier crust that Boccione uses. I love the hint of cinnamon with sour cherry jam or preserves made from Amaro cherries – or any jam that has a slightly sweet, slightly sour flavour – mixed with the rich ricotta cheese. You can also use chunks of chocolate in place of the jam.

SERVES about 12

INGREDIENTS

For the crust
100g (½ cup) sugar
170g (1½ sticks) unsalted butter, at room temperature
2 large egg yolks
200g (1½ cups) all-purpose flour
pinch of salt

For the filling
560g (2½ cups) whole milk ricotta
4 large eggs, separated
150g (¾ cup) sugar
1 tbsp all-purpose flour
grated zest of 1 lemon
1 tsp vanilla
½ to 1 tsp cinnamon
130g (½ cup) fresh, frozen, or dried cherries, defrosted and drained if using frozen (optional)
170g (½ cup) dark chocolate broken into small pieces or chocolate chips (optional)
165g (½ cup) sour cherry jam or preserve

METHOD
To make the crust

1. Put the sugar, butter, egg yolks, flour and salt in a large bowl and either rub everything together with your fingers, or quickly pulse the ingredients in a food processor fitted with a steel blade until the dough forms a ball. Either way, do not overwork the dough. Cover in clingfilm and chill in the refrigerator for a half hour.

2. Preheat the oven to 190°C (170°C fan/375°F/gas mark 5), place the rack in the top third of the oven, and grease a 25cm (10in) springform cake tin with a removable bottom.

3. On a lightly floured surface, roll out the dough into a 33cm (13in) diameter quasi-circle. Fold the dough gently and press into the tin. Trim and flatten the edges with a knife. You want this to be quite rustic. Prick with a fork and bake for 15 minutes, then remove from the oven and set aside.

To make the filling

1. Stir together the ricotta, egg yolks, sugar, flour, lemon zest, vanilla and cinnamon with a spoon in a medium mixing bowl.

2. In the bowl of a stand mixer fitted with the whisk attachment, beat the egg whites until almost stiff peaks form, and fold gently into the ricotta mixture with all the cherries and/or the chocolate. (I like mixing the chocolate and the cherries, but if you prefer, use just one or the other.)

3. Spread the cherry preserve over the entire crust, then spoon on the ricotta mixture, smoothing over the top with the back of a spoon. Bake in the top third of the oven for 40 to 50 minutes, or until the centre is set and golden brown; or do as the Romans do, and let it get slightly burnt on the top.

JOANNA NISSIM
Knafe Cheesecake

SERVES 8 generously

STORAGE
2–3 days in an airtight container in the fridge (if it lasts that long!)

INGREDIENTS

For the topping
100g (3½oz) knafe (kataifi) pastry
50g (3 tbsp) butter, melted

For the syrup
200g (1 cup) sugar
240ml water (1 cup) water
120ml (½ cup) orange juice

For the base
170g (6oz) crushed digestive biscuits or graham crackers
110g (1 stick) butter, melted

For the filling
400g (14oz) soft cream cheese
100g (½ cup) sugar
3 tbsp rosewater
2 tsp cornflour
3 large eggs

METHOD

1. Using scissors, snip the pastry into pieces. Melt the butter in the microwave then pour over the pastry and rub it in using your fingertips. Lay the pastry out flat on a baking sheet and cook for 15–20 minutes until golden. Keep checking and turning the pastry over to ensure it does not burn. Once ready, take out and leave to one side to cool.

2. Make the syrup by adding all the ingredients to a saucepan and heating over a medium heat until the sugar dissolves. Once the syrup has thickened slightly, leave to one side and let cool.

3. To make the cake, start by lining a 23cm (9in) cake tin with greaseproof paper. In a mixing bowl, crush the biscuits and stir in the melted butter until the butter has been absorbed. Tip the biscuit rubble into a bowl and press down into the bottom of the cake tin with the back of a spoon.

4. In a separate mixing bowl, mix the cheese, sugar, rosewater, cornflour and eggs using an electric mixer until you have the consistency of double cream. Pour the mixture on top of the biscuit base and place in the oven at 180°C (160°C fan/350°F/gas mark 4) for 1 hour.

5. Once cooked and the top is golden, take it out of the oven and let it cool down. Once cooled take the cake out of the tin and pile the cooled golden knafe pieces on top. Drizzle the syrup all over the top and let it sink in.

YOTAM OTTOLENGHI
Honey and Yoghurt Set Cheesecake

No oven, no bain-marie, no cracks – this is the simplest of cheesecakes! You can make this up to two days ahead, topping with the honey and thyme just before serving if you like. It will keep in the fridge, but the base will soften with time.

SERVES 8

INGREDIENTS

500g (2 cups +2 tbsp) Greek-style yoghurt
200g (about 12) Hobnob biscuits or other oat biscuits
60g (4 tbsp) unsalted butter, melted
1½ tbsp picked thyme leaves
400g (14oz) full-fat cream cheese
40g (¼ cup + 1 tbsp) icing sugar, sifted
1 lemon (finely grate the zest to get 1 tsp)
150g (5¼oz) white chocolate, broken into 1–2cm (½–1in) pieces
60g (3 tbsp) honey

METHOD

1. Line a 23cm (9in) springform cake tin with parchment paper and set aside.

2. Line a sieve with a clean tea towel and set above a bowl. Spoon in the yoghurt, then draw up the sides of the tea towel. Squeeze the yoghurt into a ball, pressing out as much liquid as you can. You want to end up with about 340g (1⅓ cups) of thickened yoghurt. Set aside until required. The liquid can be thrown away.

3. Place the Hobnobs in a clean plastic bag and crush them finely with a rolling pin. Mix with the butter and 1 tablespoon of the thyme and spoon into the cake tin, pressing it down to form an even layer. Set aside in the fridge.

4. Whisk together the cream cheese, strained yoghurt, icing sugar and lemon zest until smooth and combined: this can be done in a stand mixer or using a hand-held mixer.

5. Next melt the chocolate. This needs to be done over a pan of barely simmering water, in a heatproof bowl which sits over the pan with the base well clear of the water. Stir the chocolate frequently for 2–3 minutes, taking care not to get any moisture into the chocolate as this will cause it to seize. Spoon the melted chocolate into the cream cheese mixture and whisk until combined.

6. Spread the cream cheese mixture over the biscuit base evenly, then refrigerate for at least 2 hours, until set.

7. When ready to serve, warm the honey in a small saucepan with the remaining ½ tablespoon of thyme leaves until thin and runny. Remove from the heat and drizzle over the cheesecake. Release the cheesecake from the tin, divide into eight slices and serve.

NIGEL SLATER
Fudgy Lemon Cheesecake

If I could have just one cheesecake (an unthinkable scenario), it would be of the deep, fudgy variety, heady with vanilla freckles, so thick and 'clarty' it sticks to the roof of your mouth. I developed such a cheesecake for the first volume of *The Kitchen Diaries* and most of my subsequent ones (sour cherry, 2011, Christmas mincemeat, 2012, and gooseberry cheesecake slice, 2018) have been riffs on that. The exception was the over-the-top white chocolate and peanut butter recipe that was, by my own admission, somewhat hardcore. Sweet, gooey and intensely sticky, it could clog an artery at twenty paces. (It's fabulous, by the way.) This recipe that follows has stood the test of time. I would never be so arrogant as to say this is the perfect cheesecake. However, it really is rather good and probably closest to what we think of when we want the quiet thud of cheesecake on the table.

SERVES 8

INGREDIENTS

70g (5 tbsp) butter
200g (7oz) Nice or digestive biscuits, or graham crackers
500g (1lb 2oz) mascarpone
200g (7oz) full-fat cream cheese
150g (5oz) golden sugar
3 large eggs plus an extra yolk
1 lemon
150ml (5fl oz) double cream
½ tsp vanilla extract

METHOD

1. Melt the butter in a saucepan. Crush the biscuits to a fairly fine powder. You can do it in the traditional way, with a plastic bag and a rolling pin, or in a food processor. Tip the biscuits into the melted butter and stir briefly till the crumbs are coated. Set the oven at 140°C (120°C fan/275°F/gas mark 1). Press two-thirds of the buttered crumbs into the base of a deep 20–22cm (8–9in) loose-bottomed springform cake tin. Set aside in a cold place to become firm. The freezer is ideal.

2. Put the kettle on. Put the mascarpone, cream cheese, sugar, eggs and extra egg yolk in the bowl of a food mixer (you will need the flat beater attachment). Finely grate the lemon zest into the cheese and sugar, then beat until thoroughly mixed. Squeeze the lemon. Fold the cream, juice of the lemon and vanilla extract into the cheesecake mix.

3. Wrap the base of the tin with foil, covering the base and sides with a single piece with no joins, then pour the cheesecake mixture into the tin. Lower the cake tin into a roasting tin. Pour enough of the boiled water from the kettle into the tin to come halfway up the sides of the cake tin. Slide carefully into the oven. Bake for 50 minutes then switch off the oven and leave the cake in place to cool.

4. When the cake has cooled, chill for a good couple of hours in the fridge. (Overnight won't hurt.) Undo the spring clip, release the cake from its tin and slide onto a plate. Press the reserved crumbs onto the sides of the cake and serve.

SARIT PACKER, ITAMAR SRULOVICH
Rose-Scented Cheesecake on a Coconut Base with Berry Compote

MAKES a 23cm (9in) cake

INGREDIENTS

For the coconut base
50g (3½ tbsp) butter
100g (⅔ cup) desiccated coconut
75g (generous 1⅓ cup) sugar
½ tsp sea salt
1 egg

For the rose-scented cheesecake
500g (1lb 2oz) full-fat cream cheese
100ml (½ cup) sour cream
200g (1 cup) sugar
zest of 1 lemon
4 eggs
1 tbsp rosewater
50g (scant ½ cup) plain flour

For the compote topping
300g (2½ cups) raspberries, plus 100g (¾ cups) extra to fold in at the end
180g (¾ cup + 2 tbsp) sugar
1 lemon, halved
1 tbsp rose water
100g (½ cup) strawberries, cut in quarters, to fold in at the end

METHOD

1. Preheat the oven to 190°C (170°C fan/375°F/gas mark 5) and line a loose-bottomed 23cm (9in) cake tin with baking parchment. Melt the butter and mix with the coconut, sugar, salt and egg until well combined. Transfer to the cake tin, smooth out and bake in the oven for 10 minutes until the coconut goes a light golden colour. Remove from the oven to cool.

2. Make the filling in a mixer with a paddle attachment, or in a bowl with a large spoon (but not a whisk). Combine the cream cheese with the soured cream, sugar and lemon zest on medium speed. Add the eggs one at a time, then gradually mix in the rosewater. Finally fold in the flour. Pour over the coconut base and bake for 30–35 minutes until the cake rises and goes a light golden brown. Remove from the oven and cool in the fridge for at least 4 hours before topping.

3. Mix 300g (2½ cups) of the raspberries in a pan with the sugar and lemon halves. Set on a very high heat, bring to a rapid boil and cook for about 3–4 minutes until the compote thickens. Remove from the heat. Take out the lemon halves and squeeze them into the compote so that you don't lose any juice, then discard. Stir in the rosewater, transfer to a bowl and chill in the fridge for at least an hour until set.

4. When you are ready to serve, gently fold the additional 100g (¾ cup) of raspberries and the quartered strawberries into the chilled compote and use to top the cheesecake (or serve on the side).

DENISE PHILLIPS
Oreo and Raspberry Cheesecake

Like most cheesecake recipes, this one is in 3 parts:
1. Raspberry sauce
2. Oreo cookie base
3. White chocolate cheesecake filling

The combination of raspberry with white chocolate is luxuriously creamy and rich, which contrasts so well with the dark Oreo base.

SERVES around 16

INGREDIENTS

For the raspberry sauce

2 tsp room-temperature water (divided)
1 tsp cornflour
200g (1¾ cups) fresh or frozen raspberries (do not thaw)
25g (2 tbsp) sugar

For the base

28 regular Oreo cookies (2 packs)
120g (1 stick) unsalted butter, melted

For the filling

170g (6oz) white chocolate, finely chopped
450g (2 cups) full-fat cream cheese, softened to room temperature
50g (¼ cup) sugar
1 tbsp plain flour
1 tsp lemon juice
1 tsp pure vanilla extract
pinch of salt
2 large eggs, at room temperature

METHOD
Raspberry sauce

1. Mix 1 teaspoon of water with the cornflour in a very small bowl. Set aside. Combine the raspberries, sugar and remaining 1 teaspoon of water together in a small saucepan over medium heat. Stir the mixture, breaking up some of the raspberries as you stir.

2. Once simmering, add the cornflour mixture. Stir well and simmer for 3 minutes. Remove from the heat and press through a fine mesh strainer to remove the seeds. Cool completely before using. Cover and store for up to 1 week in the refrigerator.

Oreo base

1. Preheat the oven to 180°C (160°C fan/350°F/gas mark 4). Line the base and sides of a square 22cm (8½in) tin with baking parchment, leaving an overhang on the sides.

2. In a food processor, pulse 28 Oreos (including the cream filling) into a fine crumb. Stir in the melted butter. Pour the mixture into the prepared tin. Pat the crumbs down into the bottom to make a thick crust. Bake for 8–10 minutes. Remove and set aside. Leave the oven on.

Filling

1. Melt the chopped white chocolate in a double boiler. Let the warm chocolate cool as you work on the other cheesecake filling ingredients.

2. Using an electric mixer, whisk the cream cheese and sugar together for about 2 minutes, until the mixture is smooth and creamy. Add the flour, lemon juice, vanilla extract, salt and eggs. Whisk again until the mixture is completely smooth. Pour in the cooled (but still liquid) white chocolate until combined.

3. Pour half of the cheesecake filling onto the base. It's ok if the base is still slightly warm. Drizzle half of the raspberry sauce all over the top. Spread the remaining cheesecake filling on top. Drizzle remaining raspberry sauce on top, then use a toothpick or knife to gently swirl everything together.

4. Bake for about 35 minutes or until the cheesecake appears set on top and the edges are lightly browned. Cool for 45 minutes at room temperature, then chill in the refrigerator for at least 3 hours before slicing.

5. To slice, lift the cake out of the tin, using the baking parchment overhang to help you. Cut into squares with a sharp knife or leave it whole and cut up as desired. For extra neat squares, wipe the knife clean between each cut. Cover and store leftover cheesecake in the refrigerator for up to 1 week.

DENISE PHILLIPS
Vanilla and Dulce de Leche Cheesecake

This vanilla and dulce de leche (toffee) cheesecake certainly has the wow factor. Make it when you have a lot of guests as it is amazingly delicious but quite rich and does serve 12 people. However, once completely cool, you can freeze it. Dulce de leche (the name means 'sweet milk') is a traditional dairy product from Argentina. It is used as a topping for ice cream or fresh fruit, like bananas, and as a filling for cakes like this cheesecake. Thick and intensely flavoured, it should be slightly warmed to make it pourable.

SERVES 10–12

INGREDIENTS

For the base
225g (8oz) digestive biscuits or graham crackers
125g (1 stick + 1 tbsp) margarine, melted

For the filling
675g (1lb 8oz) full-fat cream cheese
200g (1 cup) light brown muscovado sugar
2 tbsp vanilla extract
50g (scant ½ cup) plain flour
175ml (¾ cup) dulce de leche
2 eggs

For the toffee sauce
120g (½ cup + 2 tbsp) sugar
120g (8½ tbsp) butter
pinch of salt
100ml (¼ cup + 3 tbsp) double cream

METHOD

1. Preheat the oven to 200°C (180°C fan/400°F/gas mark 6), and line a 22cm (8½in) springform tin with baking parchment.

2. Put the digestive biscuits into a food processor and pour in the melted margarine. Press onto the bottom and 3cm (1in) up the sides of the prepared tin. Bake for 12–15 minutes or until set. Remove and set aside.

3. Using an electric mixer, whisk the cream cheese, brown sugar, vanilla extract, flour and dulce de leche together until smooth and well blended. Add the eggs one at a time and whisk briefly to combine. Pour this mixture over the cooked biscuit base.

4. Reduce the oven to 160°C (140°C fan/320°F/gas mark 3). Bake for 1 hour or until set. Turn the oven off but leave the cheesecake in the oven to cool. Remove and refrigerate for 6 hours or overnight. Unclasp or remove the cake from the tin and place onto a serving plate.

5. To make the toffee sauce, melt the sugar with 3 tablespoons of water in a small saucepan until the sugar has dissolved. Increase the heat and cook without stirring until it starts to caramelise and the sugar becomes golden brown. Remove from the heat, add the butter, salt then the cream, stirring continuously until well-blended. Set aside and cool until the caramel has cooled (about 15 minutes).

6. Pour the toffee sauce onto the cheesecake and spread evenly. To cut, run the knife under hot water, wipe it dry and cut the cake into slices. To serve the stylish way: dust the plate with cocoa powder.

JOSÉ PIZARRO
Baked Cheesecakes with Blueberries

The north of Spain is renowned for its production of milk, which of course results in plenty of cheese and dairy desserts. We call cheesecakes quesadillas. This recipe is a bestseller in Pizarro, where the fruits are selected according to what's in season – blueberries in summer, spiced quince in autumn and caramelised oranges in winter.

SERVES 6

INGREDIENTS
450g (1lb) full-fat cream cheese
125g (½ cup + 2 tbsp) sugar
1½ tbsp cornflour
pinch of salt
2 medium free-range eggs
100ml (½ cup) sour cream
icing sugar, for dusting

For the blueberries
4½ tbsp lemon juice
75g (generous ⅓ cup) sugar
225g (1¼ cups) blueberries
1 tsp arrowroot

METHOD

1. Preheat the oven to 110°C (90°C fan/230°F/gas mark ¼). Tightly wrap some foil around the base of 6 poaching rings, 7cm (3in) wide and 6cm (2in) deep, then line the base and sides with greaseproof paper. Place on a baking tray.

2. Put the cream cheese in a bowl and beat with an electric hand mixer until smooth and creamy. Beat in the sugar, cornflour, salt and eggs, then stir in the sour cream. Pour the mixture into the moulds and bake for 35–40 minutes until set, but still wobbly in the centre. The cheesecakes will continue to firm up as they cool. Remove from the oven and leave to cool. These can be chilled if you wish but are best served at room temperature.

3. For the blueberries, put the lemon juice and sugar into a small pan and leave over a low heat until the sugar has dissolved. Add the blueberries, bring to a gentle simmer and cook for 1 minute. Mix the arrowroot with 1 teaspoon cold water, stir into the fruit and cook for about 30 seconds until thickened. Transfer to a small bowl and allow to cool.

4. If you chilled the cheesecakes, remove them from the fridge 30 minutes or so before service. Gently slide them out of their moulds and carefully peel off the linking paper from the bases. Put onto serving plates and then peel away the strip of paper from the sides. Dust the tops of the cheesecakes with icing sugar, spoon the blueberries around and serve.

CLAUDIA RODEN
Spanish Cheese Pudding

This very simple and light cheese pudding from the island of Menorca is baked in a *greixonera* – the local name for an earthenware cazuela. Brossat is the fresh cream cheese made from cow's milk (the English brought dairy cows when they occupied the island) – ricotta is a good substitute. Miguel Montez Martínez, who for many years cooked in the Balearic Islands during the tourist season, gave me this recipe. Now living in his home village of Frailes in Andalusia, he is called upon to cook giant stews and paellas for hundreds of people during festivals.

SERVES 6–8

INGREDIENTS

500g (2 cups) fresh ricotta cheese
125g (½ cup + 2 tbsp) sugar
grated zest of 1 lemon
5 large eggs
butter, to grease the baking dish

METHOD

1. Blend the ricotta, sugar, lemon zest and eggs to a cream in the food processor.

2. Pour into a greased baking dish about 26cm (10in) in diameter and bake in an oven preheated to 180°C (160°C fan/350°F/gas mark 4) for about 30 to 45 minutes, or until it feels firm.

3. Serve at room temperature in the dish in which it was baked.

COOK'S TIPS

- I serve it with a fragrant honey. The honey produced in neighbouring Majorca is an orange-blossom honey.
- Dust the top with icing sugar and ground cinnamon.
- For *flaó*, a speciality of Ibiza, a similar cheese mix is used to fill a thin pastry base. It is flavoured with 3–4 mint leaves and 2–3 tablespoons of an anise-flavoured spirit (you can use pastis, ouzo or arak).
- Serve it covered with icing sugar or a drizzle of honey.

VICTORIA PREVER
Tahini and Silan Cheesecake

This delicious treat giving full-on halva vibes is super simple and made in minutes.

SERVES 12

INGREDIENTS
125g (4½oz) Lotus Biscoff biscuits
125g (4½oz) digestive biscuits or graham crackers
100g (7 tbsp) butter, melted
pinch of sea salt flakes
650g (1lb 7oz) full-fat cream cheese
100g (½ cup) sugar
2 tsp vanilla extract
175ml (¾ cup) double cream
100g (¼ cup + 1 tbsp) raw tahini
2–3 tbsp silan (date molasses)
Sesame-coated peanuts or sesame snaps or vanilla/chocolate halva

METHOD
1. Line a 20–23 cm (8–9in) springform tin with baking paper. The smaller tin will make a deeper cake with a thicker base and vice versa for the larger tin.

2. Blitz the biscuits in a food processor until they turn to crumbs. Melt the butter, add the salt, then blend again until the crumbs start to clump together. Tip the crumb mixture into the tin, then flatten into an even layer using a large serving spoon. Refrigerate while you make the filling.

3. In a large bowl, beat the cream cheese, sugar and vanilla using an electric hand mixer, in a stand mixer with the whisk attachment or with a hand whisk until combined and smooth. Add the cream and tahini, then beat again until just combined – don't overmix. Scrape the mixture onto the biscuit base, then level it out to cover the base evenly. Chill for at least 3 hours or overnight.

4. To serve, drizzle the surface with date molasses and scatter with your choice of sesame-coated peanuts, broken sesame snaps or crumbled halva, or a combination for extra flavour and texture.

COOK'S TIPS
- For best results, take the cream cheese and cream out of the fridge an hour before you want to make the cake and take care not to over mix the cheesecake mixture or it may become runny. And to be sure it sets okay, you'll need to buy the cream cheese with the highest fat content you can find – this is not the time for healthy choices. I like the mix of two types of biscuit but if you prefer one or the other stick with that.

JUDI ROSE
Citrus Cheesecake with a Kumquat Glaze

Kumquats – bite-sized cousins of tangerines and oranges – are in season throughout winter and spring. Bathed in a tangy lime glaze, they make a vibrant topping for this lovely citrus-scented cheesecake.

SERVES 10

INGREDIENTS

For the crust
120g (4oz) oat biscuits, such as Hobnobs
30g (2 tbsp) melted butter

For the filling
450g (1lb) medium-fat soft cheese
80g (3oz) sugar
30g (2 tbsp) soft butter
3 level tbsp pine nuts, optional
2 level tbsp cornflour
finely grated zest and juice of 1 lime
finely grated zest of 1 orange
2 tbsp lime cordial
3 large eggs, whisked to blend

For the topping
250g (1 rounded cup) carton creamy fromage frais or sour cream
1 tbsp sugar
1 tsp lime cordial, such as Rose's

For the glazed kumquats
225g (8oz) kumquats
85g (3oz) granulated sugar
150ml (5fl oz) water

For decorating the top
1 small orange, peeled and thinly sliced

METHOD

1. Preheat the oven to 160°C (140°C fan/325°F/gas mark 3). Put the pine nuts, if using, in the oven for 5 minutes or so to dry during the heating-up process (but don't let them colour). Butter the sides of a 20–22cm (8–8½in) springform or a square tin. Crush the biscuits to crumbs then mix with the melted butter and press into an even layer on the bottom of the tin.

2. Using an electric mixer, or a wooden spoon and a strong right arm (the food processor makes the cheese too pasty), cream the cheese with the sugar and soft butter until fluffy, then mix in the pine kernels, if using, cornflour, lime zest and juice, orange zest, cordial and beaten eggs, until smooth and creamy.

3. Turn into the tin and smooth level, then bake for 35–40 minutes or until the cake feels set and firm about 2.5cm (1in) round the edge of the tin (the centre of the cake will set as it cools down). Remove from the oven and place on a cooling tray.

For the topping

Turn the oven up to 200°C (180°C fan/400°F/gas mark 6). After 10 minutes, mix the topping ingredients together then spoon over the cake. Bake for a further 8 minutes. When quite cold, refrigerate for at least 12 hours, preferably overnight.

To glaze the kumquats

1. Cut each one into 4 slices, discarding the stalk end. Put the sugar and water in a shallow pan 20–23cm (8–9in) in diameter and heat gently, stirring, until the sugar is dissolved.

2. Add the kumquat slices in a single layer and let them bubble gently until they are soft and shiny and only about 1 or 2 tbsp of syrup remain. Leave in the pan until cold (the syrup will set like jam). Use to decorate the top of the chilled cake together with slices of orange.

JUDI ROSE
Jewelled Mini Cheesecakes with a Cinnamon Walnut Crust

A mouthwatering lemon and vanilla-infused filling studded with plump sultanas sits on a buttery cinnamon and walnut base, crowned with a luscious glazed fruit topping. Golden sugar adds a delicious hint of caramel.

Mini cheesecakes are fun to make. They're great for kids or to unleash your artistic side. They take half the time of a full-size cheesecake, look as impressive as they taste and are sure to be the star of the show as a tea-time treat or elegant after-dinner dessert.

MAKES
12 x 4cm (1½in) mini cheesecakes, or
10 x cupcake-sized ones

SERVES 8–10

INGREDIENTS
For the cinnamon walnut crust
35g (3 tbsp) butter
2 tbsp sugar
60g (½ cup) plain flour
½ tsp cinnamon
50g (½ cup) walnut halves

For the filling
60g (4 tbsp) soft butter
2 tbsp sugar
pinch of fine sea salt
½ tsp vanilla extract
225g (8oz) medium fat cream cheese
60g (⅓ cup) sour cream or Greek yoghurt
finely grated zest of 1 small lemon, unwaxed if possible
1 egg
2 rounded tbsp sultanas

METHOD

1. Preheat the oven to 200°C (180°C fan/400°F/gas mark 6). Lightly oil or butter the inside of a 12-hole silicone mini cupcake mould or a standard cup muffin tin lined with 10 non-stick paper cases.

2. First make the base. Cut the butter into roughly 2.5cm (1in) chunks and put in a food processor with the sugar, flour and cinnamon. Process until the mixture is starting to form moist clumps (20–30 seconds, depending how firm your butter is). Pulse in the nuts for 10 seconds or until finely chopped but not powdery.

3. Remove the blade then tip the dough into a mixing bowl and work together gently with your fingertips until it forms a ball. Pinch off walnut-sized pieces of the mixture and press each into the bottom and slightly up the sides of each cavity in the mould or paper cases. Each base should be about 1cm (½in) thick.

4. Bake for 8 minutes or until golden, then remove from the oven and leave to cool slightly. Turn the oven down to 160°C (140°C fan/325°F/gas mark 3) while you make the cheesecake filling.

5. Put the butter, sugar, salt, vanilla and cream cheese in a bowl and beat by hand with a fork or with an electric whisk until smooth. (A food processor makes the cream cheese too runny.) Add the sour cream or yoghurt, lemon zest, egg and sultanas and beat the filling until smooth.

6. Spoon a rounded tablespoon of the filling onto each crust (a bit more if you're using muffin tins), easiest with a small ice cream scoop. When you're done, smooth the top of each cheesecake level with the back of a teaspoon.

Continued on page 108

For the glazed fruit topping
1 tbsp cornflour
half a small can sliced peaches in fruit juice or light syrup
any or all of the following fresh fruits: raspberries, pomegranate seeds, mango, or a thinly sliced lemon
tiny sprigs of mint or lemon balm, optional but pretty

7. Bake for 20–25 minutes or until the edges are golden and the surface is lightly set. The filling will continue to set as it cools. Transfer the tin to a cooling rack and leave the cakes to cool for at least 30 minutes.

8. If using a silicone mould, run a small knife around the side of each mould, then cover with the cooling rack and flip it over to release the cheesecakes. Non-stick paper cases usually release themselves. Transfer the mini cheesecakes to a plastic container large enough to hold them in a single layer. Cover and chill until up to 3 hours before serving.

9. Up to 3 hours before you want to serve the cheesecakes, slice the fruit and arrange decoratively on each cheesecake then brush with some of the liquid from the tinned peaches. Decorate some with the sprigs of mint or lemon balm.

COOK'S TIPS
- The baked cheesecakes keep for up to two days in the fridge. The uncooked crust can be frozen in their moulds or paper cases without the filling for two weeks.
- The bottom of a small spice jar is handy for tamping the crust into an even layer before baking.

SIMON WOOD
The Ultimate Gin Cheesecake Recipe

SERVES 1

INGREDIENTS

120ml (½ cup) gin
30g (2 rounded tbsp) sugar
125g (4½oz) digestive biscuits, smashed to crumbs
40g (3 tbsp) butter, melted
zest of 1 grapefruit, 1 orange and 1 lime
juice and zest of 1 lemon
280g (10oz) cream cheese
397g can (1¼ cups) condensed milk
90ml (⅓ cup + 1 tbsp) fresh lemon juice

METHOD

1. Add 120ml (½ cup) gin to a saucepan along with the sugar and simmer to reduce by two thirds.

2. Combine the biscuit crumbs and melted butter and press into the base of a 10cm (4in) metal ring, taking care to keep it crumbly and not over bash it until it becomes dust!

3. Zest your citrus fruits and set aside. Retain a little of each for the garnish. Whisk the cream cheese and condensed milk together, then slowly stir in the lemon juice and reduced gin 'syrup'. Add in the citrus zest and mix well before pouring over the prepared base.

4. Chill everything for at least 2 hours in the fridge until set. Serve with your remaining citrus zest sprinkled on the top – and possibly, a gin and tonic!

MICHEL ROUX
Orange Cheesecake

This recipe is from Michel Roux's *Pastry: Savoury & Sweet*, **first published in 2008.**

SERVES 8

INGREDIENTS
280g (9oz) *pâte sablée* (see recipe on facing page)
4 oranges
350g (12oz) fromage frais or cream cheese
350g (12oz) curd cheese
150g (½ cup + 1 tbsp) sour cream
175g (¾ cup + 2 tbsp) sugar
4 eggs

To finish
6 tbsp low-sugar Seville orange marmalade, barely warmed and strained
candied orange peel sticks from 2 oranges (optional, see recipe on facing page)

METHOD

1. Roll out the *pâte sablée* to a round, 3mm thick, and use to line a lightly greased 20cm (8in) diameter, 4cm (1½in) deep flan ring. Chill for at least 20 minutes.

2. Preheat the oven to 170°C (150°C fan/325°F/gas mark 3). Prick the base of the pastry case. Bake the case blind for 30 minutes. Remove the beans and paper and return to the oven for 5 minutes, then set aside to cool. Lower the oven setting to 140°C (120°C fan/275°F/gas mark 1).

3. For the filling, finely grate the zest from the oranges, then squeeze the juice and strain through a chinois. Put the soft cheeses, sour cream and sugar in a large bowl and mix thoroughly with a spatula. In another bowl, whisk the eggs until frothy, then delicately incorporate them into the cheese mixture. Add the orange zest and juice and mix with the spatula until evenly combined.

4. Pour the filling into the pastry case and bake in the low oven for 1½ hours. To check that the cheesecake is cooked, insert a fine skewer into the centre; it should come out clean. Place on a wire rack and leave for about 20 minutes before removing the flan ring. Let cool completely, then place in the least cool part of your fridge until ready to serve.

5. To serve, carefully spread an even layer of marmalade over the surface of the cheesecake. Wait a few minutes for the glaze to set, then cut the cheesecake into portions using a very sharp knife. Serve on individual plates, with confit orange peel sticks, drizzled with a little of their syrup, on the side if you like.

Pâte sablée

MAKES
about 650g (1lb 7oz)

INGREDIENTS
250g (2 cups) plain flour
200g (1¾ sticks) butter, cut into small pieces and slightly softened
100g (1 scant cup) icing sugar, sifted
pinch of salt
2 egg yolks

METHOD
1. Heap the flour on the work surface and make a well. Put in the butter, icing sugar and salt. With your fingertips, mix and cream the butter with the sugar and salt, then add the egg yolks and work them in delicately with your fingertips.

2. Little by little, draw the flour into the centre and work the mixture delicately with your fingers until you have a homogeneous dough.

3. Using the palm of your hand, push the dough away from you 3 or 4 times until it is completely smooth. Roll it into a ball, wrap in clingfilm and refrigerate until ready to use.

Candied citrus peel sticks

MAKES
enough for 6–8 servings

INGREDIENTS
2 grapefruits or large oranges
400g (2 cups) sugar

For coating the candied peel (optional)
50g (2 tbsp) coarse-grained sugar

METHOD
1. Using a sharp, flexible knife, cut off a 5mm (¼in) sliver from the base and top of the fruit. Starting from the top and following the contour of the fruit, cut off 5 bands of peel, 3cm (1in) wide and 6cm (2in) long, from each fruit (including the pith). Cut each band into 3 strips, each 1cm (½in) wide.

2. Put the strips in a saucepan, cover with cold water and bring to the boil. Refresh, drain and repeat the operation twice more.

3. Pour 300ml water (1 cups + ¼ cup) into a saucepan, add the sugar and heat slowly to dissolve the sugar, then bring to the boil. As soon as the syrup boils, drop in the blanched citrus peel sticks and cook gently for 1½ hours.

4. Leave the citrus sticks in the syrup until barely warm, then lift out onto a wire rack and leave to drain until cold. If you wish, roll them in the granulated sugar. Store in an airtight container and use within 3 days.

CARMEL SARANO
Rhubarb and Custard Cheesecake

INGREDIENTS

For the stewed rhubarb (to be made at least 4 hours in advance)
400g (2 cups) rhubarb cut into 2cm (½in) pieces
rind and juice of 1 medium orange
50g (¼ cup) sugar

For the base
30g (2 tbsp) butter
150g (5oz) ginger biscuits, crumbled into a fine crumb

For the cheesecake mixture
550g (1lb 3½oz) full-fat cream cheese
3 medium eggs
100g (½ cup) sugar
1½ tbsp cornflour

METHOD
Stewed rhubarb
Place the ingredients in a bowl and cover. Set aside for 30 minutes to macerate. After 30 minutes, tip everything into a saucepan, bring to boil then simmer for 10–15 minutes until all the fruit is cooked. Next turn the heat up for 5 minutes to evaporate most of the liquid – you'll need to continuously stir at this point. Leave to cool while you prepare the base and filling.

Base
Melt the butter in a pan, then stir in the biscuit crumbs. Pour the coated crumbs into a cake tin, and using a spoon, compress the crumbs until you are left with an even base layer. Bake in oven at 175°C (150°C fan/350°F/gas mark 4) for 5–8 minutes.

Cheesecake mixture
1. Whip together all the cake ingredients in a large bowl. Once whipped, roughly remove half the mixture into another bowl.

2. In bowl 1, add ½ of a vanilla pod or 1 teaspoon vanilla extract and stir together. In bowl 2, add 100g (½ cup) of cold rhubarb, removing as much 'extra' liquid as possible – don't sieve, you need some liquid! Add 1 tablespoon cornflour. Stir together.

3. Cover the base with a thin layer of cake mixture from bowl 1, then add spoonfuls of the mixture from bowl 1 and bowl 2 on top until both bowls have been emptied.

4. Bake in the oven for 30 minutes. After baking is complete, slightly open the oven door enough to jam open with a wooden spoon. Leave the cake in the oven for 4–6 hours before placing in the fridge for another 5 hours. Serve at room temperature.

SHERI SILVER
Raspberry Cheesecake Hamantaschen

The perfect Purim mash-up, with a tangy raspberry cheesecake flavour running through the dough, filling and topping.

SERVES 24

INGREDIENTS

For the dough
- 50g (¼ cup) sugar
- 85g (3oz) cream cheese, at room temperature
- 115g (1 stick) unsalted butter, at room temperature
- 1 large egg, at room temperature
- 1 tsp vanilla
- 160g (1¼ cups) all-purpose flour
- 140g digestive biscuits (9 full-sheet graham crackers), processed into fine crumbs
- ¼ tsp kosher salt or fine sea salt
- 40g (1½oz) freeze-dried raspberries

For the filling
- 50g (¼ cup) sugar
- 150g (5oz) cream cheese, at room temperature
- few drops of vanilla extract
- 3 tbsp raspberry jam

Before baking
- egg wash (made with 1 egg beaten with 1 tbsp water)
- raw sugar, for sprinkling

METHOD

1. Make the dough. Beat the sugar, cream cheese and butter until light and fluffy. Add the egg and vanilla and beat again. Scrape down the sides of the bowl and add the flour, 120g (1 cup) of the biscuit crumbs and the salt (reserve the leftover crumbs). Beat until incorporated. Add 120g (1 cup) of the raspberries and beat until just combined (reserve the leftover raspberries).

2. Divide the dough into two discs and roll each 0.6cm (¼in) thick between two sheets of parchment paper. Chill until firm (at least 1 hour and up to three days).

3. To make the filling, beat the sugar, cream cheese and vanilla until light and fluffy. Set half the mixture aside. Use a disposable pastry or ziplock bag and alternate small spoonfuls of the cream cheese mixture with the raspberry jam. Snip a small opening in the bottom.

4. Place one of the parchment sheets of dough onto a baking sheet. Remove the top sheet and cut out 5–6cm (2–2½in) circles, removing the trimmings. Pipe ½ teaspoon-sized mounds of the filling onto the centre of each circle. Fold the dough into a triangle, pinching the corners firmly. Brush with the egg wash and sprinkle with the raw sugar. Repeat with the remaining sheet of dough, and then again with the dough trimmings. Place the hamantaschen in the freezer for at least 15 minutes (and up to overnight).

5. Preheat the oven to 175°C (155°C fan/350°F/gas mark 4). Bake the hamantaschen for 15 minutes, or until golden brown. Remove to a wire rack to cool completely.

6. Warm the reserved cream cheese mixture until runny. Place the remaining raspberries in a ziplock bag and crush with a rolling pin. Use a spoon to drizzle the cream cheese mixture over the hamantaschen, then sprinkle with the reserved graham cracker crumbs and crushed raspberries. Chill until set.

COOK'S TIPS

As for creating the perfect no-leak, keeps-its-shape hamantaschen, here are some of my tried-and-true tips:

- Roll the hamantaschen dough ½cm (¼in) thick – a thinner dough won't keep its shape.
- Pipe no more than ½ teaspoon of filling into each hamantaschen. It won't seem like nearly enough, but as the filling expands when the hamantaschen bake, starting with less will ensure that the sides don't get pushed out and leak out onto your baking sheet.
- Egg wash is key – it's the 'glue' that keeps the hamantaschen together, so don't skip this step.
- Chill the unbaked hamantaschen in the fridge for at least 1 hour and up to 3 days, or freeze for 15 minutes or up to 12 hours. This step will ensure your hamantaschen will keep their shape each and every time.

VIVEK SINGH
Shrikhand Cheesecake with Fennel and Coriander Strawberries

This dessert has been a classic at Cinnamon Club over the years. It's a great example of bringing together the best of both worlds, combining rich Indian shrikhand of hung yoghurt and cardamom with a fresh chaat of strawberries, a quintessential British favourite when in season. Giving shrikhand a cheesecake treatment takes this dessert to another level.

SERVES 4

INGREDIENTS

For the crumble base
250g (2 cups) plain flour
250g (1¼ cups) sugar
180g (1½ cups) ground almonds
250g (2¼ sticks) cold salted butter, diced

For the filling
250g (1 cup) strained Greek yoghurt made from 500g (2 cups) of yoghurt that is left to drain overnight
100g (⅔ cup) mascarpone cheese
100ml (¼ cup + 3 tbsp) double cream, whipped to soft peaks
50g (¼ cup) sugar
½ tsp ground cardamom

For the fennel and coriander flavoured strawberries
250g (1½ cups) strawberries, hulled – some sliced and some left whole (or use any other berries in season)
grated zest and juice of half a lime
2 mint leaves, finely shredded
1 tsp fennel seeds, roasted and crushed
1 tsp coriander seeds, roasted and crushed
pinch of salt
pinch of sugar

METHOD

1. To make the crumble base, mix together the flour, sugar and ground almonds, then rub in the butter until the mixture resembles coarse crumbs. Spread on a baking tray lined with greaseproof paper and bake in an oven preheated to 180°C (160°C fan/350°F/gas mark 4) for 10–12 minutes, until golden brown.

2. Remove from the oven and leave to cool, then use your fingertips to break into fine crumbles.

3. For the cheesecake filling, gently fold together all the ingredients and chill for 20 minutes.

4. To assemble the cheesecake, press a layer of the crumble about 1.5cm (½in) thick in a 15cm (6in) springform cake tin. Add the cheesecake mixture, smooth the surface and place in the fridge to chill for at least 2 hours.

5. Meanwhile, prepare the strawberries. Put the strawberries in a non-metallic bowl, add the remaining ingredients and toss gently. Leave to macerate for 10–15 minutes.

6. Slice or scoop the cheesecake onto serving plates and serve with the strawberries dotted around. In the restaurant, we add strawberry caramel tuile.

ED SMITH
Honeyed Basque Cheesecake

The burnished, Basque-style cheesecake has become something of a food media darling in recent years. Indeed, I wondered if it was too clichéd and of the moment to include a version here. However, this is the only kind of baked cheesecake I enjoy, and I'm certain that when it stops being 'a thing', it will still be deliciously satisfying in its cream-cheesy, bronze-top-yet-wibbling-middle way. It's also very easy* to make (essentially: mix the ingredients, put them in the oven and burn).

So here is 'my' version, which is emboldened with honey to a level that should support rather than dominate the dairy; although it's still worth saying that the more characterful the honey, the better the end result. This is delicious with poached or roasted seasonal fruit like rhubarb, quince, pears and plums, but also excellent on its own.

*You could make this by hand and elbow grease, but the recipe assumes you have a stand mixer.

SERVES 8

INGREDIENTS

butter, for greasing the tin
600g (1lb 5oz) full-fat soft cheese (without additives or stabilisers – check the ingredients)
120g (½ cup + 2 tbsp) golden sugar
4 large eggs
300ml (1¼ cups + 1 tbsp) double cream
2½ tbsp good-quality raw runny honey
scant ½ tsp flaky sea salt
40g (⅓ cup) plain flour, sifted

METHOD

1. Butter the base and sides of the cake tin, then line with baking paper to leave 4–5cm (1½ –2in) of paper above the edges of the tin. The paper doesn't need to be neat; a rippled fluting is fine.

2. Collate and measure all the ingredients before starting. Heat the oven to 220°C (200°C fan/425°F/gas mark 7) and set a rack a touch higher than the middle, ensuring the tin and its high-sided lining will fit.

3. Load the mixing bowl of a stand mixer with the soft cheese and sugar. Use the paddle attachment at medium speed to beat and cream everything together until the sugar is fully incorporated (it'll take about 2 minutes).

4. Keep the mixer at a medium pace and break the eggs in one by one, adding the next only once the previous egg is fully incorporated. (Tip: crack each egg first into a bowl then tip that into the machine to avoid spending time fishing shells out the cake mix.)

5. Pause. Scrape the sides down, then return the mixer to medium speed and add the cream, honey and a pinch of salt. Allow the machine to keep beating the mix for 1 minute more, then slow it right down (but don't turn it off) and sprinkle in the flour one tablespoon at a time. Increase the speed to medium again for a final 60 seconds, then pour the custardy batter into the lined tin.

6. Place the filled cake tin on a baking sheet and slide into the oven for 40 minutes if you'd like a slightly gooey centre; 45 minutes if the priority is a browned top. Whichever you choose, at that moment remove the puffed-up and burnished cheesecake from the oven and leave to completely cool (and sink), before serving at room temperature or below.

7. This keeps well for 2 days if covered and stored in a cool place or the fridge.

MEERA SODHA
Vegan Baked Vanilla Cheesecake

SERVES 8

INGREDIENTS

100g (1 cup) shelled walnuts
100g (1 cup) shelled pistachios
30g (2 tbsp) unsalted vegan butter, melted
2 tbsp agave or brown rice syrup
⅛ tsp sea salt
750g (1lb 10oz) vegan cream cheese – I like Sheese
300g (1 cup) silken tofu, drained (290g drained weight – just under 1 cup) – I like Clearspring
150ml (½ cup + 1 tbsp) vegan double cream
200g (1 cup) sugar
1 tsp ground vanilla beans, or 1½ tsp vanilla extract
30g (3 tbsp) cornflour
zest of 1 lemon

METHOD

1. Heat the oven to 220°C (200°C fan/425°F/gas mark 7). Cut out a 38cm x 38cm (15in x 15in) square of greaseproof paper and push it into a 20cm (8in) springform cake tin (pan), flattening it against the sides and pressing it down and over the top edge.

2. Put the nuts and melted butter in a food processor, add the syrup and salt, then pulse to a coarse crumb – don't work it for too long, otherwise it will turn into nut butter. Tip the nut mix into the tin, scraping out the food processor really well, and use the back of a tablespoon to press it evenly all over the base of the tin.

3. Put the vegan cream cheese, tofu, cream, sugar, vanilla, cornflour and lemon zest in the food processor bowl and blitz to a smooth cream. Pour this evenly over the nut base, then bake for 50 minutes, turning the tin once halfway through. After this time, the cheesecake should have some blackened patches on top and a gentle wobble.

4. Remove, leave to cool to room temperature, then refrigerate for at least five hours, or overnight, until properly fridge cold. Slice and serve.

COOK'S TIP

- Not all vegan cheeses are created equal. It's very important here to use one that's made with both coconut and soy. I recommend a good quality supermarket own brand. Don't use Violife: I tried it, and it doesn't work in this recipe.

TESTER'S TIP

- We made it with a digestive biscuit/vegan butter base because I'm allergic to pistachios.

MICHAEL SOLOMONOV
New School Konafi

MAKES
12 individual cakes

INGREDIENTS

For the filling
680g (2¾ cups) ricotta cheese
3 tbsp unsweetened cocoa powder
140g (1 cup) chopped dark chocolate (at least 60% cocoa)

For the konafi
175ml (¾ cup) double cream
100g (½ cup) sugar
450g (1lb) kataifi, cut crosswise into 2.5cm (1in) long pieces
2 x lemon syrup (see below)
240g (1 cup) labneh

For the lemon syrup
400g (2 cups) sugar
240ml (1 cup) water
juice and grated zest of 2 lemons

METHOD
Filling

1. Place the ricotta and cocoa powder in the bowl of a stand mixer fitted with the paddle attachment and beat on medium speed until combined.

2. Melt the chocolate over a double boiler. Stream the chocolate into the ricotta–cocoa mixture with the mixer on low speed. Mix until incorporated. Refrigerate.

Konafi

1. Combine the cream and sugar in a small saucepan over medium heat and bring to a simmer. Cook, stirring, until the sugar is dissolved, about 2 minutes. Refrigerate until chilled.

2. Place the kataifi and the cream–sugar mixture in a bowl and stir gently until evenly combined. Divide half of the kataifi mixture between 12 oiled ramekins, 9cm (3½) in diameter by 5cm (2in) deep. Use parchment paper to push the kataifi flat. Refrigerate for 1 hour.

3. Preheat the oven to 190°C (170°C fan/375°F/gas mark 5). Using an offset spatula, spread the filling evenly over the kataifi. Spoon the remaining half of the kataifi mixture evenly over the top, cover with oiled parchment, and gently press until the top layer is flat and even, then remove and discard the parchment.

4. Bake until golden brown, about 50 minutes. Cool on a wire rack. Drizzle with lemon syrup (see below), pop out of the ramekins and serve with labneh.

Lemon syrup

Combine the sugar with the water in a medium saucepan over a high heat and bring to a boil. Continue boiling, whisking, until the sugar is completely dissolved, about 2 minutes. Add the lemon zest and juice and cover. Let stand off the heat for 15 minutes. Strain out and discard the zest. Reserve the syrup.

MARLENA SPIELER
Classic American Creamy Cheesecake

There are a million cheesecake recipes, including ones that are topped with fruit or scented with lemon, but this classic is the most tempting. It makes the perfect dessert for a bar or bat mitzvah or family meal, or as a standby to keep in the freezer.

INGREDIENTS

130g (1 stick + 1 tbsp) butter, melted, plus extra for greasing the tin
350g (12oz) digestive biscuits or graham crackers, finely crushed
350–400g (1¾–2 cups) sugar
350g (12oz) full-fat soft white (farmer's) cheese
3 eggs, lightly beaten
15ml (1 tbsp) vanilla extract
350g (1½ cups) sour cream
strawberries, blueberries, raspberries and icing sugar, to serve (optional)

METHOD

1. Butter a deep 23cm (9in) springform tin. Put the biscuit crumbs and 4 tablespoons of the sugar in a bowl and mix together, then add the melted butter and mix well. Press the mixture into the prepared tin to cover the base and sides. Chill for about 30 minutes.

2. Preheat the oven to 190°C (170°C fan/375°F/gas mark 5). Using an electric mixer, food processor or wooden spoon, beat the cheese until soft. Beat in the eggs, then 250g (1¼ cups) of the sugar and 2 teaspoons of the vanilla extract.

3. Pour the mixture over the crumb base and bake for 45 minutes, or until a cocktail stick, inserted in the centre, comes out clean. Leave to cool slightly for about 10 minutes. (Do not turn the oven off.)

4. Meanwhile, combine the sour cream and remaining sugar, to taste. Stir in the remaining vanilla extract. When the cheesecake has cooled, pour over the topping, spreading it out evenly. Return to the oven and bake for a further 5 minutes to glaze.

5. Leave the cheesecake to cool to room temperature, then chill. Serve with a few fresh strawberries, blueberries and raspberries, dusted with icing sugar, if you like.

VARIATIONS

- To make a strawberry cheesecake, in place of the sour cream, mix together 130g (generous 1 cup) fresh strawberries, sliced, with 30–45ml (2–3 tablespoons) melted redcurrant jelly. Spread the mixture over the top of the cheesecake and return to the oven until warmed through. Leave to cool, then chill before serving.
- For a lemon cheesecake, instead of the vanilla extract, flavour the cheesecake with the grated zest and the juice of 1 lemon.

EMMA SPITZER
Israeli White Chocolate Cheesecake

I make this cheesecake a lot. I make catering size trays of it for parties and it never fails to receive a chorus of praise from the lucky recipients. It's a no-bake cheesecake which means there is little that can go wrong, just ensure that you use good quality cream cheese and don't substitute the biscuits – they are the key ingredient. This needs no other accompaniment other than some nice fresh raspberries to cut through the sweetness. It's rich and velvety and incredibly moreish – eat with caution.

SERVES 6–8

INGREDIENTS

For the biscuit base
200g (7oz) Petit Beurre biscuits
120g (1 stick) unsalted butter, melted

For the filling
150g (5oz) white chocolate, broken into pieces
200g (1¾ sticks) unsalted butter, softened
125g (½ cup + 2 tbsp) sugar
1 large egg plus 1 large egg yolk
250g (9oz) good-quality cream cheese (I recommend Philadelphia)
200g (¾ cup + 2 tbsp) full-fat crème fraîche
fresh raspberries, to serve (optional)

METHOD

1. For the biscuit base, blitz the biscuits to crumbs in a food processor, then mix with the melted butter. Alternatively, place them in a freezer bag and bash with a rolling pin to make crumbs, then mix with the melted butter in a bowl.

2. Press two-thirds of the mixture into a 20 x 27cm (8 x 11in) baking dish, flattening it out so that it forms an even layer. Place in the freezer for 15 minutes until set.

3. Meanwhile, prepare the filling. Put the chocolate pieces in a heatproof bowl and either set over a saucepan of gently simmering water (ensuring the bottom of the bowl doesn't touch the water underneath) and leave until melted, or heat in the microwave on medium in 30-second bursts, until melted, stirring after each burst. Leave to cool slightly.

4. While the chocolate is melting and cooling, beat the softened butter, sugar, whole egg and egg yolk together in an electric stand mixer fitted with the paddle attachment until fluffy (or in a bowl with a wooden spoon and develop some muscle at the same time!); this will take around 10 minutes.

5. Beat the cream cheese and crème fraîche together in a separate bowl, then stir in the melted chocolate. Add to the butter and sugar mixture, then carefully fold the ingredients together.

6. Spread the mixture evenly over the biscuit base and top with the remaining biscuit crumbs. Refrigerate for a minimum of 3 hours – but 24 hours is preferable. Serve in slices with fresh raspberries to accompany, if you like. Refrigerate any leftovers in the dish covered with clingfilm for up to 3–4 days.

RICK STEIN
Baked Vanilla Cheesecake with Blueberry Topping

The following recipe is brand new! It comes from *Rick Stein's Food Stories* cookbook, which was published in September 2024. It is Rick's 31st bestselling cookbook.

SERVES 8–10

INGREDIENTS

140g (1 stick + 2 tbsp) butter, melted, plus extra for greasing the tin
280g (2⅓ cups) digestive or ginger nut biscuits
500g (1lb 1½oz) full-fat cream cheese
300g (1¼ cups) sour cream
150g (¾ cup) golden sugar
3 large eggs, beaten
4 tsp vanilla extract

For the blueberry topping
300g (1½ cups) blueberries
65g (⅓ cup) sugar
juice of ½ lemon
4 tsp cornflour

METHOD

1. Grease and line the base of a 23cm (9in) springform cake tin. Put the biscuits in a plastic bag and bash with a rolling pin until they resemble breadcrumbs. Tip them into a bowl and mix with the melted butter, then transfer to the cake tin. Press and flatten the mixture with the back of a spoon, then cover and refrigerate for 30 minutes.

2. Preheat the oven to 160°C (140°C fan/320°F/gas mark 3). Put the cream cheese, sour cream, sugar, eggs and vanilla extract into a large bowl and, using an electric hand whisk, beat until smooth. Pour the mixture on top of the chilled biscuit base.

3. Bake the cheesecake for 50–60 minutes until just set, then leave it to cool in the oven with the door ajar for 30 minutes. Transfer to the fridge to chill for 3–4 hours.

4. Meanwhile, make the blueberry topping. Put the blueberries, sugar, lemon juice and 100ml (¼ cup + 3 tablespoons) of water in a pan, place over a medium heat and slowly bring to the boil. Mix the cornflour to a paste with a tablespoon of water, add this to the blueberries and cook for a couple of minutes until the mixture starts to thicken. Leave to cool fully and then refrigerate.

5. Run a sharp knife around the edge of the tin to loosen the cheesecake, then slide it onto a plate. Spread the blueberry topping over the top of the cheesecake or slice the cake and spoon some of the blueberry mixture over each portion. Serve immediately.

ADEENA SUSSMAN
Boozy Cheesecake Milkshake

MAKES
1 large or 2 small milkshakes

INGREDIENTS
1 pint (2 cups / 570ml) premium vanilla ice cream
60g (2oz) cream cheese
60ml (¼ cup / 2oz) chilled vodka
1½ teaspoons vanilla bean paste or extract
¼ teaspoon fine sea salt
3 digestive biscuits or graham crackers, or 5 Biscoff biscuits, crumbled, plus more for garnish
whipped cream to add to the top of the milkshake (optional)

METHOD
1. Chill a large metal cup (or glass) in the freezer.
2. Combine all ingredients in a blender and blend until smooth.
3. Transfer to the glass and garnish with crumbled Biscoffs.
4. Top with whipped cream (optional).

ERAN TIBI
Eran's White Chocolate Cheesecake with Banana Compote

This cheesecake is very special to us as it was the first cheesecake we introduced when we opened Bala Baya and is still our favourite.

INGREDIENTS

For the cheesecake
600g (1lb 5oz) cream cheese
300g (1¼ cups) sour cream or Greek yoghurt
grated zest of 1 orange
1 tsp vanilla extract
5 medium eggs
600g (1lb 5oz) white chocolate, melted
250g (1½ cups) white chocolate chips

For the banana compote
1kg (2lb 3oz) bananas, each cut into 4 pieces
30g (2 rounded tbsp) light brown sugar
10g (2 tsp) unsalted butter
125ml (½ cup) banana liqueur
1 litre (4 cups + 3 tbsp) orange juice, freshly squeezed
2 tsp vanilla paste

For the tahini crumble
200g (¾ cup) tahini
½ tsp baking powder
200g (1¾ sticks) butter
80g (¼ cup + 2 tbsp) sugar
750g (6 cups) plain flour

METHOD

Cheesecake filling

Beat the cheese, sour cream or Greek yoghurt, orange zest and vanilla in a mixer. Slowly add the eggs, while still beating, until combined. Fold the melted white chocolate into the mix followed by the chocolate chips. Place in the fridge until the crumble base is ready and cooled.

Banana compote

Place the bananas in a baking tray. Mix the rest of the ingredients together and pour over the bananas. Place in the oven at 240°C (220°C fan/500°F/gas mark 9) for 5 minutes or until bananas have caramelised on top. Leave aside to cool.

Tahini crumble

1. Place all the ingredients in a bowl and mix together by hand until it has formed a dough. To keep the dough nice and short, the less you work it the better.

2. Press down onto a baking tray to an even thickness 2.5cm (1in) thick and bake at 160°C (140°C fan/325°F/gas mark 3) for 15–20 minutes. Take out of the oven and allow to cool. Once cool, crush into a coarse crumble with your hands.

Assemble and bake the cheesecake

1. Preheat the oven to 150°C (130°C fan/300°F/gas mark 2). Line the bottom and sides of a 28cm (11in) tart case with baking parchment and fill the base of the case with a layer of the tahini crumble about 1cm (½in) deep. Add the cheesecake mix on top of the crumble so it reaches the top of the tart case.

2. Bake in the oven for 40 minutes, then turn the oven up to 180°C (160°C fan/350°F/gas mark 4) and bake for another 20 minutes, until slight cracks appear on top. It needs a panna cotta wobble when it comes out.

3. Take out of the oven and allow to cool. When cooled, portion the cheesecake and spoon the banana compote on top of each serving, along with a drizzle of raw tahini.

OFER VARDI
Strudel's Distant Cousin

Hungarians boast that there is no such thing as a recipe for *vargabéles* (varga-BELL-esh): either you know how to bake it, or you don't. Since this dish was first released from its pan 100 years ago, just about every home cook in Hungary has made it at one time or another – with a recipe or without one.

A distant relative of rétes or strudel, *vargabéles* is composed of two layers of fragile, almost-transparent puff pastry, sandwiching a fat pile of thin noodles. The noodles are covered in soft, sweet cheese, flavoured with vanilla and dotted with raisins. Some cooks prefer to roll the pastry together with the filling, as in a typical strudel.

The *vargabéles* is a native of Transylvania, from back in the days when the region was in Hungarian territory. It's named after a man named Varga, who owned a small restaurant in the city of Kolozsvár. Perhaps it was the sour cheese that he made from scratch, or maybe the transparent noodles he kneaded with his own two hands – all we know for sure is that in Budapest, to this day, they sigh and say: Varga's *vargabéles* just can't be replicated. People say the dish was so tasty that even during the Second World War, with cannons thundering in the background, aeroplanes transported slices of *vargabéles* from far-flung Kolozsvár to bread-starved Budapest.

INGREDIENTS

300g (10oz) thin egg noodles
50g (4 tbsp) butter, melted
4 eggs, separated
50g (4 tbsp) butter, softened
seeds from 1 vanilla pod
150g (1¼ cups) icing sugar
500g (1lb 1oz) pressed cottage cheese, drained
400ml (scant 1¾ cups) sour cream
100g (½ cup + 3 tbsp) raisins
grated zest of 1 lemon
butter, for greasing the pan and brushing on top of the pastry
2 sheets of ready-rolled puff pastry, about 450g (1lb) total
60g (½ cup) breadcrumbs
icing sugar, to serve

METHOD

1. Cook the noodles according to the packet instructions until soft. Rinse, drain and place in a bowl. Add the melted butter, mix well, and set aside. Preheat the oven to 180°C (160°C fan/350°F/gas mark 4).

2. Prepare the filling: place the egg whites in a bowl and beat to stiff peaks. In a separate large bowl, combine the softened butter, egg yolks, vanilla seeds and icing sugar, and whisk to a light batter. Add the cheese, sour cream, raisins and lemon zest, and mix well. Add the cooked noodles and mix. Gently fold in the whipped egg whites.

3. Assemble the dish: grease a 28 x 18cm (11 x 7in) baking tin or dish with butter and line with a sheet of puff pastry. Brush well with melted butter and sprinkle with an even layer of breadcrumbs. Pour the filling on top and cover with the remaining pastry sheet. Generously brush with butter and bake until golden, 25–35 minutes. Allow to cool for 10 minutes before dusting with icing sugar.

COOK'S TIPS

- Try adding various fruits to the filling such as cherries, plums and apricots.
- The filling can be substituted with a savoury one: stir together 500g (2 cups) pressed cottage cheese, 2 egg yolks, 400ml (1¾ cups) sour cream, a chopped onion, 1 crushed garlic clove, finely chopped dill, chives, parsley and salt. Fold in 2 whipped egg whites and place on the sheet of puff pastry in the pan.

LOUISA WALTERS
Jo's Mum's Cheesecake

I was a late convert to cheesecake. The first time I ever tried it was at my husband's Grandma Dora's weekly Shabbat tea. She was a wonderful baker with a true lightness of touch, but hers was a no-bake cheesecake. Being newlywed and somewhat unsure of my skills in the kitchen, this was something I felt brave enough to try. For years it was my centrepiece of choice, until the day I was at my friend Jo's son's first birthday tea, whereupon she presented a showstopper of a cheesecake that was everything mine wasn't. It was square where mine was round, it was tall where mine was flat, it was golden yellow where mine was white, and it was baked where mine was not. This was in fact Jo's mum's cheesecake, and that is what it is called on the dog-eared, stained recipe in my recipe folder. I have refined it slightly over the years, so it is now Louisa Walters' cheesecake, but I like the nostalgia that comes with the original name. So here, in honour of Grandma Dora and Jo's mum, I am sharing with you Jo's mum's/Louisa Walters' cheesecake.

INGREDIENTS

360g (12oz) digestive biscuits, crushed and mixed with 30g (2 tbsp) melted butter
3 large eggs
225g (1 cup + 2 tbsp) sugar
¾ tsp vanilla extract
2 tsp custard powder
juice of half a lemon
150ml (⅔ cup) double cream
680g (1lb 8oz) cream cheese

For the topping
300ml (1½ cups) sour cream mixed with 2 tsp sugar

METHOD

1. Preheat the oven to 160°C (140°C fan/325°F/gas mark 3). Line a large 23cm (9in) loose-bottomed round or square tin with the biscuit and butter mixture.

2. Whisk the eggs and sugar together. Add the vanilla, custard powder, lemon juice and cream, then add the cream cheese and whisk for a minute or two.

3. Pour the mixture over the base and bake for approximately 40 minutes. Take out of the oven and allow to cool. It will split, but don't worry, because when it's cool, you can cover the top with sour cream and hey presto, it looks perfect!

4. Refrigerate overnight but serve at room temperature.

JOSHUA WEISSMAN
Homemade NYC Cheesecake

New York-style cheesecake is the easiest and most delicious dessert you can make at home. With a few simple techniques and a topping of homemade strawberry jam, you can have one of the smoothest and creamiest desserts in the game.

INGREDIENTS

For the crust

160g (5½oz) digestive biscuits or graham crackers, finely crushed
2 tbsp sugar
1 tsp kosher salt or fine sea salt
few grinds ground nutmeg
56g (4 tbsp) unsalted butter, melted

For the cheesecake filling

900g (2lb) cream cheese, softened
220g (1 cup) sugar
4 whole eggs
1 egg yolk, separate
60ml (¼ cup) double cream
57g (¼ cup) crème fraîche
2 tsp vanilla extract
pinch of salt
2 tbsp cornflour

For the strawberry jam

450g (3 cups) strawberries, sliced in half
110g (½ cup) sugar

METHOD
Crust

1. Preheat the 180°C (150°C fan/350°F/gas mark 4).

2. In a medium bowl, mix together the crushed biscuits, sugar, salt, and optional grated nutmeg. Mix in the melted unsalted butter until thoroughly combined.

3. Generously grease a 23cm (9in) springform tin with oil and dump in the biscuit mixture. Using a flat bottom cup, press the crumble into a firm even surface. Bake for 8 minutes. Remove from the oven and allow to cool completely.

Cheesecake filling

In a large mixing bowl, beat together the cream cheese and sugar. When creamed, blend in the eggs one at a time, followed by the egg yolk. Once the egg is fully incorporated, whisk in the cream, crème fraîche, vanilla, salt and cornflour.

Strawberry jam

1. Start by slicing off the top of the strawberries and cutting them into halves or quarters. Place into a medium-size saucepan. Add the granulated sugar. Mix together and let sit for 15 minutes.

2. Set over a stove set to medium heat. Allow to boil for 10 minutes and stir occasionally, until the strawberries melt and the liquid releases. Remove 80ml (⅓ cup) of the mixture and add to a blender. Blend until smooth. Add back to the rest of the strawberries and mix them together.

For the leftover cheesecake balls
leftover cheesecake
185g (1¼ cups) all-purpose flour
55g (¼ cup) sugar
1 tsp baking powder
1 tsp salt
240ml (1 cup) whole milk
oil
icing sugar, for dusting

Assembly

1. Pour the filling onto the completely cooled crust. Cover the tin with foil and place into the bottom of a roasting dish. Pour enough boiling water into the roasting dish to come 2.5cm (1in) up the side of the tin.

2. Place in the oven at 160°C (140°C fan/325°F/gas mark 3) for 1½ hours until set but slightly jiggly. Once it's done, open the oven door and let it sit in the water bath in the oven for 45 minutes. Remove and place onto a wire rack to cool the rest of the way.

3. Once cooled completely, cover with clingfilm and chill overnight and up to 2–3 days. Carefully remove the cheesecake from the springform pan and place on a board to cut. Top with the strawberry jam and serve.

Leftover cheesecake balls

1. Take the leftover cheesecake, remove the crust and cut into 4cm (1½in) cubes. Place on a tray and freeze until solid.

2. In a medium bowl, add and combine the flour, sugar, baking powder and salt. Whisk together. Whisk and stream in the whole milk until smooth.

3. Take a frozen cheesecake cube, dunk it into the batter, and drop into a small pan of 180°C (350°F) oil. Fry for 3–4 minutes, flipping occasionally. Drain on a wire rack set over a baking sheet. Serve with a dusting of icing sugar.

ITTA WERDIGER
Cheesecake de Provence

SERVES 12–14

INGREDIENTS

For the crust

80g (5½ tbsp) butter
1 pinch dried culinary lavender flowers
80g (¼ cup + 2 tbsp) organic sugar
3g (½ tsp) salt
1g (1¾ cups + 1 tbsp) ground almonds
70g (½ cup) flaked almonds

For the cheese custard filling

50g (⅓ cup) arrowroot starch (or any starch)
170g (⅔ cup) double cream
680g (1lb 8oz) cream cheese
pinch of salt (or more if your cream cheese is not salted)
250g (1 cup) sugar
2 tsp bourbon vanilla bean extract
450g (2 cups) sour cream
5 eggs

For the topping

65g (¾ cup) flaked almonds
pinch of salt
1 tbsp fruity flavourful olive oil + more for drizzling
2 tbsp honey
pinch of culinary lavender flowers

METHOD

1. To make the crust, melt the butter on the stove in a medium pan. Once the butter is melted, turn off the heat and add all the rest of the crust ingredients one at a time, stirring between each addition. Transfer the mixture to a 23cm (9in) springform tin lined with baking parchment or greased with butter or spray. Pat into an even layer and leave to cool.

2. For the filling, whisk the arrowroot and cream until smooth. Place into the bowl of a food processor, add the the remaining filling ingredients one at a time and keep mixing. Make sure there are no lumps before adding the eggs, so the eggs don't get over beaten. Pour the mixture into the tin over the now-cooled almond crust.

3. Place in the middle of the oven and bake at 180°C (150°C fan/350°F/gas mark 4) for 50 minutes or until the edges seem firm and the middle is still quite wobbly. Turn the oven off and leave the cheesecake in overnight or until cooled. Place in the fridge the next day if you have time – it's not a must, but it will be easier to transfer.

4. For the topping, mix together the ingredients, then lay on a baking tray and pop it in the oven for about 10 minutes at 170°C (150°C fan/350°F/gas mark 4) or until brown. For a more even colour, remove the tray after about 5 minutes, toss the nuts around and reposition them using a spatula, then continue to cook. Once the nuts have cooled, pile them on top of the cooled cheesecake. Drizzle more fruity olive oil over the top.

5. Optional Candied Lavender Syrup: take a few spoons of lavender, 100g (½ cup) sugar and 120g (½ cup) water and boil it on the stove for 10 minutes until it becomes a light syrup. When cooled, strain half over the cake, then keep cooking the lavender until the syrup thickens, then pour it over greased parchment paper. When cold and set, crumble some of the candied lavender on top of the almonds.

COOK'S TIPS
- Never trust a springform pan! I always wrap the bottom in foil.
- I use pasture-raised eggs, organic sugar and dairy from grass-fed cows. Better for our bodies and the earth.
- This recipe is versatile and can be made with other styles of fresh cheese. I learnt from my mother to adjust the amount of liquid and starch to compensate for a more watery cheese (like quark).
- Don't overbeat the eggs, either do them by hand or add them to your machine last. Overbeating creates a soufflé effect and leads to cracking.

CALLAN WENNER
Ube Cheesecake

SERVES 12

INGREDIENTS

For the coconut crust

280g (2 cups) digestive biscuits or graham crackers

50g (¼ cup) sugar

30g (½ cup) unsweetened coconut flakes

¼ tsp fine sea salt or kosher salt

110g (1 stick) unsalted butter, melted

For the cheesecake batter

900g (2lb) full-fat cream cheese, at room temperature

200g (1 cup) sugar

30g (¼ cup) cornflour

100g (⅓ cup) ube halaya (purple yam jam)

4 eggs, at room temperature, whisked

1 tbsp vanilla

230g (1 cup) full-fat sour cream, at room temperature

1–2 tsp ube extract

METHOD

Preheat the oven to 180°C (150°C fan/350°F/gas mark 4). Prepare a 23cm (9in) springform tin by adding a piece of parchment paper to the bottom of the pan and clipping it in (cut excess off around the edges). Then spray the sides with nonstick cooking spray and add 2–3 strips of parchment paper along the sides to cover it completely. I like to have mine come just above the lip of the tin.

Coconut crust

1. Pulse the biscuits, sugar, coconut and salt until fine and sandy. Add the melted butter and pulse until all crumbs are completely moistened.

2. Add the crumbs to the springform tin and use a small measuring cup to press into the bottom and sides. Start by pushing the crumbs to the sides and pressing them about three quarters of the way up the pan. Then, press down in the centre until it's completely compacted.

3. Bake for 10 minutes, then transfer to a wire rack to cool while you make the cheesecake layer. Lower the oven to 150°C (130°C fan/300°F/gas mark 2) and add an empty casserole dish to the bottom rack of the oven. Set a pot of water to boil and pour into the casserole dish once boiling.

Cheesecake batter

1. Add the softened cream cheese to the bowl of a stand mixer fitted with the paddle attachment (or use a hand mixer) and mix on low until it's broken down and creamy. Scrape down the sides.

2. Mix together the sugar and cornflour in a bowl, then add to the cream cheese and mix on low until fully combined. Add the ube halaya and mix again until evenly distributed.

3. Crack the eggs into a separate bowl and whisk to break down. Add the vanilla into the eggs. With the mixer running on low speed, drizzle the eggs into the batter and mix until fully incorporated.

Continued on next page

For the coconut whipped cream
unsweetened coconut flakes, lightly toasted
400ml (1½ cups) coconut milk, refrigerated
30g (¼ cup) icing sugar
½ tsp vanilla
80ml (⅓ cup) whipping cream, cold

4. Scrape down the sides one more time, then add the sour cream and mix on low until incorporated. Add the ube extract and mix again to deepen the colour (and flavour). Use a rubber spatula to mix one more time by hand to remove any air bubbles. Tap it on the counter a few times then let it sit for about 5 minutes.

5. Pour the cheesecake batter into the crust and use your spatula to smooth it out to meet the edges. Bake on the centre rack for 1 hour 45 minutes. Turn off the oven and crack it open slightly for 1 hour. Transfer the cheesecake to a wire rack and cool at room temperature for 30 minutes. Finally, transfer to the fridge (uncovered) and chill for at least 8 hours.

Coconut whipped cream

1. Add the coconut flakes to a frying pan set over a medium heat and toast until lightly browned, tossing every 15 seconds. Transfer to a plate to cool completely.

2. Open the can of coconut milk and remove some of the cream. Pour out all the liquid (reserving for another use), then add all of the solidified cream to a bowl. Add the icing sugar and vanilla and use a stand mixer (with the paddle attachment) or hand mixer to break down the coconut cream until it's smooth and creamy.

3. Switch to a whisk attachment (if using a stand mixer). Add the whipping cream and mix on low to combine, then increase the speed and whip on medium-high speed until light and fluffy and peaks form. Dollop, spread, or pipe the whipped cream on top of the chilled cheesecake, then top with toasted coconut flakes before serving.

COOK'S TIPS

- When cutting the cheesecake, wipe the knife off completely between each slice or else the cheesecake can stick to the knife and pull away.
- Store the cheesecake covered in the fridge for up to one week. The whipped cream will start to weep after 3–4 days. Feel free to leave off the whipped cream and allow guests to add their own whipped cream to slices.

SHLOMI ZIV
New York Cheesecake with Pomegranate

INGREDIENTS

For the syrup
3 tbsp pomegranate seeds
zest from half a lime
120ml (½ cup) water
100g (½ cup) sugar

For the base
200g (7oz) digestive biscuits or graham crackers
50g (3½ tbsp) butter, melted

For the filling
750g (1lb 10½oz) cream cheese
250g (1 cup) sour cream
3 tbsp double cream
200g (1 cup) sugar
6 medium-sized eggs
1 tbsp vanilla paste
1 tbsp pomegranate molasses

For the topping
300g (1¼ cup) sour cream
30g (generous ¼ cup) icing sugar
fresh pomegranate seeds and lime zest, to garnish

METHOD

1. Start by preparing the syrup. In a small saucepan, bring all the ingredients to a boil, then lower the heat. While occasionally stirring, mash the pomegranate seeds. Cook until a thick syrup is formed. Allow to cool completely.

2. For the base: grind the biscuits in a food processor. Add the melted butter. Press into the bottom of a 24cm (9in) diameter tin and refrigerate for at least one hour.

3. Mix all the filling ingredients together, except for the pomegranate molasses. Divide the batter into two parts. Add the pomegranate molasses to one part of the batter. Pour the white batter over the biscuit base, and add the second batter, one tablespoon at a time, swirling with a knife or wooden skewer.

4. Bake in a preheated oven at 160°C (140°C fan/325°F/gas mark 3) for 45–60 minutes, until the edges are set and the centre is still slightly wobbly. Remove from the oven and allow to cool completely.

5. Prepare the topping. Mix the sour cream and icing sugar together then spread over the almost-chilled cake. Refrigerate overnight.

6. Shortly before serving, drizzle the cold pomegranate syrup you prepared over the cake, and garnish with fresh pomegranate seeds and lime zest.

Glossary of UK–US Terms

Baking sheet	Unrimmed cookie sheet
Baking tin	Sheet pan or jelly roll pan
Bicarbonate of soda	Baking soda
Biscuits	Cookies
Bramley apples	Use a mix of Braeburn, Granny Smith, Northern Spy or Winesap
Bread flour	All-purpose flour
Cake tin	Cake pan
Caster sugar	Granulated or superfine sugar
Clingfilm	Plastic wrap
Cocktail stick	Toothpick
Coriander (fresh)	Cilantro
Cornflour	Cornstarch
Dark chocolate	Plain chocolate
Double cream	Heavy cream
Enamelled casserole	Dutch oven
Extra-strong bread flour	Bread flour
Foil	Aluminum foil
Flaked almonds	Almond slices
Ground almonds	Almond flour
Icing sugar	Confectioners' or powdered sugar
Plain flour	See note on UK and US flour (below right)
Skimmed milk	1% milk
Self-raising flour	Self-rising flour
Sieve	Strainer
Single cream	Light cream
Sultanas	Golden raisins
Tin	Can

A Note on Measurements

Both UK metric and imperial or imperial US cup measurements are included in these recipes for your convenience. Conversions are approximate and may have been rounded up or down. It is important to follow one set of measurements only and not alternate between them within a recipe, as they are not interchangeable.

All spoon measurements are level. 1 teaspoon is 5ml; 1 tablespoon is 15ml. As the difference in volume is so small between US and UK spoon measures, we have assumed British and American spoons to be interchangeable but some adjustment in the quantity of seasonings may be necessary to suit individual tastes.

Butter is salted, unless unsalted is specified. Margarine is a soft variety labelled 'high in polyunsaturates', unless a block of firm margarine is specified.

Unless specified, eggs are medium (UK) = large (US) – approximately 50g (2oz) in weight. Note that large eggs (UK) = extra-large (US). The egg size is only critical when 4 or more eggs are used in a recipe; in that case extra-large (or small) eggs can upset the ratio of liquids to solids.

Sugar is UK white caster (US granulated or superfine) unless otherwise specified, such as icing sugar (US powdered or confectioners'), or soft brown, golden or demerara sugar.

Cake-tin sizes are given for guidance only, and those of approximately the same size can be used, provided they are the same depth or deeper than specified.

A Note on UK and US Flour

Flour is UK plain unless all-purpose flour is specified. UK 'plain flour' is made with soft wheat and contains less protein than North American 'all-purpose flour'. It also absorbs less liquid.

For recipes that use plain flour, readers in North America should use a combination of ⅔ all-purpose and ⅓ cake flour for best results.

For recipes that use all-purpose flour, readers in the UK should expect to use slightly less liquid.

Contributors

Nadine Abensur
Nadine Abensur is the author of seven vegetarian cookery books, including *The Cranks Bible* and *Enjoy*. Nadine ran a vegetarian catering company in London for many years and was then Food Director of the vegetarian chain Cranks. She moved to Australia in 2002, wrote another book or two and then opened an art gallery, which she ran for 11 years. After many years of not daring to, she has now taken up painting. You can visit her website nadinesfeast.com

Sherry Ansky
Sherry Ansky is a highly acclaimed Israeli chef and author of cookbooks such as *Food of Israel: Authentic Recipes from the Land of Milk and Honey*.

Mary Berry
Mary Berry is one of Britain's most well-known and highly acclaimed food writers, chefs and television presenters. She has published more than 75 cookery books and has hosted several television series, including *The Great British Bake Off* until 2016.

The Bull & Last
Located near Hampstead Heath in North West London, The Bull & Last is an historic pub founded by directors Freddie Fleming, Ollie Pudney and Joe Swiers.

Martyne Burman
Despite Martyne's family being a mix of Ashkenazi and Sephardi, her mother cooked very English food. It wasn't until Martyne left home that she discovered how spices and herbs could transform food into something that delights and surprises. A love affair had begun. Fortunately for Martyne, others liked her food, too, and she was able to change a hobby into a successful catering business. You can see more at thecookingcrew.com

Linda Dangoor
Linda Dangoor was born in Baghdad, Iraq. She's a designer, painter and ceramicist, and now also a food writer. She has worked in the design field for many years creating products for the gift market in Paris and London. Linda is the author of two cookbooks. The first one, *Flavours of Babylon*, is an exploration and a celebration of the flavours and recipes of her Baghdadi heritage. Her second book, *From the Tigris to the Thames*, is about food and belonging and will be published in 2025. You can follow her on Instagram at @lindadangoorcreativeliving and Twitter @lindadangoor or visit her website lindadangoor.com

Aviva Elias
Aviva Elias was born in Singapore, at a crossroads of distinct and assimilated exotic cuisines. Thus began her cosmopolitan food journey and innate curiosity to experience the world, which has not dimmed. Ever inquisitive, she ventured across five continents tasting and learning how best to combine flavours, colours and textures. She brought these together in her company Saffron, catering events in London and further afield for more than 20 years.

Becky Excell
'Queen of Gluten Free' Becky Excell is a seven times *Sunday Times* best-selling author and a trusted authority on all things gluten-free, with a following of over one million on her social media channels.

Becky is an advocate for positive change for the gluten-free and free-from community through her best-selling cookbooks and regular national TV appearances and as a proud ambassador for Coeliac UK. Nobody should have to miss out just because they must follow a gluten-free diet. She's also passionate about shining a light on the cost of living for those who are gluten free to ensure that gluten-free food is affordable and accessible to all those who need it.

Not only have her cookbooks received Nigella

Lawson's seal of approval, but Becky was also awarded *Observer Food Monthly*'s Best Food Personality award in 2022, the Creator Award's Food Creator of the Year 2022 and BBC Food Creator of the Year 2023. You can find her on social media @beckyexcell and visit her website at glutenfreecuppatea.co.uk

Hugh Fearnley-Whittingstall
Hugh Fearnley-Whittingstall is a writer, broadcaster and campaigner. His recent BBC One series *Easy Ways to Live Well*, alongside comedian Steph McGovern, looked at our perceptions of healthy eating and wellbeing. Hugh's Channel 4 series has earned him a hugely popular following, while his *River Cottage* books have collected multiple awards including the Glenfiddich Trophy and the André Simon Food Book of the Year. Hugh's additional broadcasting, like the hugely influential *Fish Fight*, has earned him a BAFTA as well as awards from Radio 4, *The Observer* and the Guild of Food Writers. Hugh lives in Devon with his family. You can find him @hughfearnleywhittingstall / @rivercottage / rivercottage.net

Tracey Fine and Georgie Tarn (The Jewish Princess)
Tracey Fine and Georgie Tarn were both inspired by their grandmother's and mother's balabusta capabilities. Lifelong friends, their common denominator was always food, family and friendship, and they would often cook together for the Jewish holidays.

In 2005, inspired by their mutual passion for Jewish food and lifestyle, they created a new, modern, comedic cookbook called *The Jewish Princess* – a cross between *Sex in the City* meets *Desperate Housewives* meets Jewish food. To date, they have published four books: *The Jewish Princess Cookbook*, *The Jewish Princess Feasts and Festivals*, *The Jewish Princess Guide to Fabulosity* and *The Modern Jewish Table*.

They have also made several television appearances and talked about kosher cookery across the radio airwaves in the UK, Spain and America, including interviews on BBC, LBC and REM. Their upbeat, entertaining Princess Positive look on life, family, food and friendship brings fun, style and a dash of chutzpah to the kitchen.

Badannie Gee
Based in North London, Piped Dreams Bakery was the brainchild of TV producer Badannie Gee. From an early age, Badannie loved baking birthday cakes for all her family and friends, and after having children of her own, she would spend her weekends and evenings baking for her children's friends. Demand for her artistic creations has grown so much that she now works full time, darting between baking celebration cakes and teaching cake decorating to adults and children.

Ravneet Gill
Ravneet Gill is one of the UK's leading pastry chefs, an author, an activist and a television presenter. In 2020, she replaced Prue Leith to work as a judge on *Junior Bake Off* alongside Liam Charles and Harry Hill. She is the author of *The Pastry Chef's Guide*, *Baking for Pleasure* and *Sugar, I Love You*. In spring 2025, she launched her debut restaurant, Gina.

Stuart Gillies
Stuart Gillies is a highly acclaimed British chef. After training in the UK, he spent a year in Rome and three years in Stockholm. He then moved to Daniel's in New York City to work under Daniel Boulud. On returning to the UK, he worked at Le Caprice in London before joining Angela Hartnett as head chef at The Connaught and opening the Gordon Ramsay-owned Boxwood Café in May 2003. Stuart was chef director at the reopened Savoy Hotel from October 2010, and also at Plane Food. He has appeared on BBC One's *Saturday Kitchen* and competed in the second series of *The Great British Menu*.

Galit Goldstein Orlow
Born in 1977 in Israel, Galit has called Zurich home since 2008, where she lives with her husband, Alain, and their two children, Ilai and Shir. As a passionate confectioner she shares the flavours of her hometown, Tel Aviv, through her baking atelier. Inspired by her mother, who made Aliyah from Egypt, she finds joy in creating nostalgic treats that evoke cherished memories. The kitchen has always been at the heart of her life, filled with happiness and family traditions. For her, cooking and baking are both an art and a science, and each dish she creates is infused with love, aiming to delight those who experience her creations. Witnessing their joy is the most rewarding part of her culinary journey.

Helen Graham
Helen is a food writer living in London, specialising in vibrant vegetable-forward Middle Eastern-inspired food. She was previously the executive chef of Bubala, where

she helped to establish the brand and grow it to two sites. The restaurant received much critical acclaim and quickly became a favourite for vegetarians and meat eaters alike. Helen has also worked at some of the capital's best Middle Eastern spots, including The Barbary, Ottolenghi and The Palomar.

Ainsley Harriott
One of the country's favourite TV chefs for nearly 30 years, Ainsley Harriott is a household name on the British culinary scene. He trained at Westminster College and has had a long career working in top London hotels, restaurants and professional kitchens, amassing a wealth of culinary experience. In 2020, he was awarded an MBE for his services to broadcasting and the culinary arts.

Mark Hix
Mark Hix is frequently lauded as one of Britain's most eminent restaurateurs with an unrivalled knowledge of ingredients with provenance. He is an award-winning author and food writer with 12 cookbooks to his name, the latest of which, *Hooked*, regales stories of fishing from his childhood through to the present day. Previously a regular contributor to *City AM* and *GQ*, Mark was also the food writer for *The Independent on Saturday* for 14 years. He now has a regular column in *The Telegraph*, *Dorset Magazine* and *Marshwood Vale* and a weekly cookery show on Lyme Bay Radio. He was recently appointed Director of Food and Drink at London's Groucho Club.

Angela Hartnett
Angela Hartnett is an English Michelin-starred chef and one of the most highly acclaimed chefs and restaurateurs in the UK. Her career as a chef has taken her all over the world and has made her a well-known TV personality. She was Chef-Patron at Angela Hartnett at The Connaught in London and is currently Chef-Patron at Murano and Café Murano in London and at Cucina Angelina in Courchevel, France. She was awarded an OBE in 2021 for her services to the hospitality industry and to the NHS during the Covid-19 pandemic.

Ken Hom CBE
Ken Hom is a renowned Chinese-American chef, author and television presenter who specialises in Chinese cuisine. His nearly 40 cookbooks and his own range of Ken Hom Woks have inspired millions of people around the world to try cooking Asian food themselves.

Gil Hovav
Gil Hovav is a leading Israeli culinary journalist, author, restaurant critic and TV personality. He has been a huge proponent of Israeli cuisine and has played a major role in encouraging a greater appreciation of the country's cuisine. He has created some of Israel's most popular TV cooking shows and has written a number of bestselling cookbooks and novels.

Ian Hughes
Ian Hughes is a graphic designer working within all genres of publishing and has been involved with book design since leaving Ravensbourne College of Art and Design many years ago. He was art director (for 16 years) at one of the UK's leading publishers, before setting up his own business in 2001 – Mousemat Design Limited. He has designed and typeset well over a thousand books throughout his career, for many high-profile authors. When relaxing, he enjoys cooking. Particularly the bit when you put on some French lounge jazz and open a bottle of wine from the southern Rhône valley.

Clarissa Hyman
Clarissa Hyman is an award-winning food, travel and culture writer based in Manchester. She has written five books, including *The Jewish Kitchen*, and co-authored a compilation of seasonal autumn and winter recipes, based on her columns in *Food and Travel* magazine.

Anne Iarchy
Anne began baking out of boredom at the beginning of lockdown. She started with all the desserts she was going to bake 'one day when she'll have time'. Soon she discovered sourdough and challah, and started taking her bakes to the Friday night family get-togethers. Over the past few years, she expanded her baking skills, from bread to cakes and biscuits and regularly bakes for family and friends. Towards the end of 2023, she was diagnosed as coeliac and had to start baking everything gluten free. Anne is not willing to compromise on taste and texture when it comes to gluten-free bakes. She also runs online gluten-free baking classes. You can follow her journey and hear more about her classes on instagram @little_home_baker

Rukmini Iyer

Rukmini Iyer is the author of *The Roasting Tin* series, selling over 1.75 million copies worldwide. She has a popular weekly recipe column in *The Guardian* and writes for numerous publications, including *OcadoLife*, *BBC Gardener's World Magazine*, *Waitrose Food* and her Substack *At the Table*. She makes regular appearances cooking live on BBC's *Saturday Kitchen*, and her latest book, *The Green Cookbook*, on easy weeknight dinners, is out now.

Lizzie Kamenetzky

Lizzie is an English-born food stylist, writer and cookbook author with a natural flare and passion for beautiful food and fantastic recipes. Her great love of food started at an early age, learning to cook with her mum who taught her not only about how to create delicious dishes but about how great food brings people together, providing not only sustenance but happiness, comfort and joy. She also learnt from an early age about both the pleasures of growing your own produce and about the provenance of what we eat, from field to fork.

Lizzie has worked for many top publications, including six years as Food Editor of the award-winning food title *delicious*. Now she works freelance as a food writer, stylist, cookbook author and ghost writer.

Kirsten Kaminski

Kirsten Kaminski is the creator behind the social media platform *The Tasty K* – a recipe video blog featuring healthy plant-based recipes, exclusive travel guides and drool-worthy photography that will inspire you to get creative in the kitchen and lead a healthier, more conscious lifestyle. Since 2016, when Kirsten started her blog, she has gained more than half a million followers on Facebook and Instagram and more than 50 million organic video views, with thousands of people trying her delicious recipes.

Josh Katz

Josh Katz is the critically acclaimed chef behind – and co-owner of – three London-based restaurants: Berber & Q, Shawarma Bar and Carmel. Before opening his first self-owned restaurant Berber & Q in 2015, he worked in some of the most renowned kitchens in London, including the likes of Galvin Bistrot de Luxe, Ottolenghi and Zest. Josh is also the published author of two cookbooks: *Berber & Q: The Cookbook* and *Berber & Q: On Vegetables*.

Tom Kerridge

Tom Kerridge, the award-winning and celebrated chef, brings a taste of culinary magic to his restaurants, cookbooks and across TV screens up and down the country. A Gloucestershire lad, Tom champions British food and suppliers and has become a leading name in the hospitality industry. From humble beginnings, Tom and his wife, Beth, built The Hand & Flowers into what it is today, the world's first and only two Michelin-starred pub. Tom has since launched several more restaurants, penned ten best-selling cookbooks, launched the hugely successful music and food festival *Pub in the Park* and more recently he campaigns to help end child hunger in the UK with Full Time meals.

Sivan Kobi

Born in Israel, Sivan relocated to Los Angeles at a young age, where she still lives today with her husband, children and grandchildren. For a decade, she ran a home-based business specialising in intricately designed custom-made tiered cakes. However, when the pandemic hit, her passion for sharing recipes and her love for cooking blossomed even further, leading her to discover a new avenue for expression as a content creator on Instagram.

Leah Koenig

Leah Koenig is the author of seven cookbooks including the acclaimed *The Jewish Cookbook* and *Modern Jewish Cooking* and the recently published *Portico: Cooking and Feasting in Rome's Jewish Kitchen*.

Leah's writing and recipes can be found in *The New York Times*, *New York Magazine*, *The Wall Street Journal*, *The Washington Post*, *Food & Wine*, *Epicurious* and *Food52*, among other publications. She also writes a weekly newsletter, *The Jewish Table*, which shares recipes and stories from the world of Jewish food.

In addition to writing, Leah leads cooking demonstrations and workshops around the USA and the world. She lives in Brooklyn, New York, with her husband and two children.

Pierre Koffmann

Pierre Koffmann is a French professional chef who was one of a small number of chefs in the UK to be awarded three Michelin stars at his restaurant La Tante Claire in London.

Kim Kushner

Culinary educator Kim Kushner is the best-selling author

of *The Modern Table*, *I Heart Kosher*, *The New Kosher* and *The Modern Menu*. Raised in Montreal, Canada, Kim learnt to cook at an early age from her Moroccan-born mother and later graduated from the Institute of Culinary Education in Manhattan. Kim travels the world teaching her wildly popular cooking classes. Kim has appeared on the *Today* show and has been featured in *The New York Times International Edition*, *Saveur*, *Huffington Post* and *The Chicago Tribune*, and is recognised as a leader in redefining kosher cuisine. Her cookbooks feature everyday recipes for delicious and artful dishes made from accessible, seasonal ingredients. Kim lives in New York City with her husband and children.

Marie Laforêt
Marie Laforêt is a photographer, culinary writer and vegan food consultant who specialises in vegan cuisine. Since the launch of her blog *100% Végétal*, she has published 20 vegan cookbooks including the bestselling *Vegan Bible* and *Incredible but Vegan*.

David Lebovitz
David Lebovitz is a NYC-born professional chef and author, a household name in the culinary world. He spent over a decade at Chez Panisse in California before leaving the restaurant business in 1999 to write books and moving to Paris in 2004. He is the author of several books, including *The Perfect Scoop*, *Ready for Dessert*, *The Great Book of Chocolate*, *The Sweet Life in Paris* and *Drinking French*. He has also been featured in many highly regarded culinary publications.

Sharon Lurie
Sharon Lurie is the author of the award-winning *Kosher Butcher's Wife* series, including *Cooking with the Kosher Butcher's Wife*, *Celebrating with the Kosher Butcher's Wife* and *A Taste of South Africa with the Kosher Butcher's Wife*. She is a kosher product creator and has a range of salad dressings under the name 'Bobba Shar's salad dressing'. She is the Food Editor of *Jewish Life* magazine, has a radio show on Chai FM radio and contributes articles to the local and international media.

Sarah Mann-Yeager
Sarah Mann-Yeager is a wife, mother, and gin connoisseur. She is a sometime journalist, full-time butcher, baker and candlestick maker. She has been cooking for as long as she can remember, kneeling up on a kitchen stool in her grandma's kitchen. She is a food tourist, and her palate stretches around the globe. She flinches at the term 'cultural food appropriation', as she is a child of the diaspora. We take our food heritage and make it with the ingredients available wherever we end up; using the raw materials of where we live is not appropriation, for without them, we would starve. Travel broadens the mind and wakes up the palate to new and exciting flavours that can and should be incorporated into our lives. She works full time running the family business. To see her full bio and more recipes, visit louismann.co.uk

Gill Meller
Gill Meller is a chef, food writer, food stylist and cookery teacher. For more than 15 years, he has been part of the River Cottage team, working closely with Hugh Fearnley-Whittingstall to source ethically produced and sustainable food and serve up some truly delicious dishes. He has been featured regularly on the Channel 4 series *River Cottage* and has appeared at various food shows and festivals in the UK and further afield. Gill regularly writes for publications such as *The Guardian*, *The Observer* and *delicious.* magazine. He is also the author of a number of award-winning cookbooks, including *Root, Stem, Leaf, Flower: How to Cook with Vegetables and Other Plants* and *Outside: Recipes for a Wilder Way of Eating*.

Thomasina Miers
When Thomasina Miers first arrived in Mexico aged eighteen, she fell so in love with its food that she went back to live there, opening a cocktail bar and cooking with some of Mexico's top chefs. After returning to London and winning BBC's *MasterChef* in 2005, Thomasina co-founded Wahaca, winner of numerous awards for its food and sustainability credentials. Tommi's passion lies in great food and how it can positively affect people and the environment: she co-founded the 'Pig Idea' campaign in 2015 and in 2017, she helped set up Chefs in Schools. An ambassador for the Soil Association, she was awarded an OBE in 2019 for her services to the food industry. Tommi has a weekly column in *The Guardian*'s *Feast* magazine. She lives in London with her husband and three daughters.

Hannah Miles
Hannah Miles was a high-flying legal eagle before launching into her highly successful career as a home cake-maker and baker, reaching the finals on *MasterChef*,

where judge John Torode said, "Hannah is one of the most naturally gifted cooks I have seen in a long time." She is the author of many beautiful books including *Cake Pops* and *Microwave Mug Cakes!*

Monday Morning Cooking Club (Lisa Goldberg, Merelyn Frank Chalmers and Natanya Eskin)

The Monday Morning Cooking Club is a group of irrepressible Sydney women who curate, document and preserve recipes from Jewish kitchens across Australia and the world. Their four best-selling cookbooks honour and celebrate treasured family recipes, alongside moving stories of family, friendship, community and survival. Their books are sold all over the world and they have created an engaged online community of home cooks.

Yanir Mrejen

Yanir Mrejen is a remarkable, imaginative chef who has worked in the world's leading restaurants alongside famous chefs such as Gordon Ramsay. He helped to launch the Glatt Kosher meat and fish restaurant Novellino Bistro in London and works closely with the Brighton & Hove Jewish Community Centre (BNJC). He lives in Brighton and Hove with his family.

Silvia Nacamulli

Silvia Nacamulli is a London-based cook, lecturer and author specialising in Italian Jewish cuisine. A well-recognised name on the international food and cooking circuit she grew up in Rome, surrounded by her home country's passion for food. She is a regular columnist for *The Jewish Chronicle* and the author of *Jewish Flavours of Italy: A Family Cookbook*. You can follow her on Instagram @Silvia_Nacamulli or cookingforthesoul.com

Joan Nathan

Joan Nathan, known as the 'Jewish Julia Child', is the author of thirteen cookbooks, including *Jewish Cooking in America* and *The New American Cooking*, both winners of James Beard and IACP Awards. Her latest books, *My Life in Recipes* and *A Sweet Year*, explore Jewish food and tradition. She is a regular contributor to *The New York Times*.

Joanna Nissim

Joanna Nissim is a passionate food writer, recipe developer, cookery teacher and general foodie. She loves to cook everything but especially her family's Sephardic recipes. She also hosts demonstrations and private cooking lessons from home and within the community. She loves to write for various publications and has written a cookbook of her family recipes, which she hopes to publish in the near future. Her recipes and handy tips can be found on her Instagram page: @joanna_nissim

Yotam Ottolenghi

Yotam Ottolenghi is a highly acclaimed Israeli-born British chef, restaurateur and author. He is the co-owner of eight hugely successful Ottolenghi delis and restaurants across London. He is also the author of a number of best-selling, award-winning cookbooks, including *Ottolenghi: The Cookbook, Plenty, Jerusalem* and *Simple*.

Sarit Packer and Itamar Srulovich

Pursuing a long-held ambition to open their own Middle Eastern-inspired restaurant, chefs Sarit Packer and Itamar Srulovich opened Honey & Co. in June 2012 in central London. They have since added a deli, Honey & Spice, a grill house, Honey & Smoke, and a café-bakery, Honey & Co. Daily. The couple has also published four cookbooks: *Honey & Co. Food from the Middle East*, winning *Sunday Times* Food Book of the Year, *Honey & Co. The Baking Book, Honey & Co. at Home* and *Chasing Smoke: Cooking Over Fire Around the Levant*. They host a podcast, *Honey & Co.: The Food Sessions*, winner of Fortnum & Mason Podcast of the Year, inviting interesting and influential guests from the food and drink industry for a chat, and also write a recipe column for *FT Weekend Magazine*.

Denise Phillips

Denise Phillips is one of the UK's leading Jewish chefs and cookery writers with seven popular books to her name, the Denise's Kitchen Cookery school (jewishcookery.com) and the highly original Date on a Plate cookery classes for singles. In addition, she is a regular contributor to *The Jewish Chronicle, The Jewish Weekly* and other publications.

José Pizarro

Spanish-born José Pizarro is an award-winning chef and bestselling author who has lived in London for 26 years. He runs highly acclaimed restaurants in London, Surrey and Abu Dhabi.

Victoria Prever

Victoria Prever is the food editor at *The Jewish Chronicle*, having left a legal career to train as a professional chef at Leith's School of Food and Wine. Since then, she has worked as a food critic for *The Ham and High*, as a private caterer and taught at cookery schools (including Leith's and Good Housekeeping). On top of this, she is a freelance food writer, regularly contributing to *Good Food* magazine, and a food consultant, working with various food brands.

Claudia Roden
Claudia Roden is an Egyptian-born British writer of cookbooks and a cultural anthropologist. She is the author of several bestselling Middle Eastern cookbooks, including *A Book of Middle Eastern Food*, *The New Book of Middle Eastern Food* and *Arabesque: Sumptuous Food from Morocco, Turkey and Lebanon*.

Judi Rose
Cookbook author, chef and cookery teacher, Judi is the daughter of legendary Jewish food writer Evelyn Rose, MBE. Raised in England, Judi has lived in New York, Dallas, Italy and Israel and is an expert in deliciously healthy international home cooking and culinary techniques. The author of several cookbooks, most recently *To Life! Healthy Jewish Food*, she also runs bespoke boutique cooking classes at Judi's Cookery Studio in West London. Visit her at judirose.com

Michel Roux
Michel Roux OBE (1941–2020) was French born and remains one of the most highly respected chefs and restaurateurs in the world. In 1967, he and his brother, Albert, opened the legendary Le Gavroche in London, the first to receive three Michelin stars in Britain and taken over by Albert's son, Michel Jnr, in 1991, before closing its doors in 2024. In 1972, the brothers opened The Waterside Inn at Bray-on-Thames that has held three Michelin stars since 1985, the longest in the world outside France. Michel's son, Alain, succeeded his father as Chef Patron in 2001 and in 2023 opened the Alain Roux Culinary School and Michel Roux Library to continue to elevate the Roux legacy.

Carmel Sarano
Carmel is passionate about food, always has been. She's a mother of three and recipe developer. In the past couple of years, she's been producing reels for Kosher Kingdom and Shefa Mehadrin. Recently, Carmel opened a PTSD weekly workshop for victims of terrorism in Israel, her other passion.

Sheri Silver
Sheri Silver is a food photographer, recipe creator and food stylist based in NYC. In addition to writing her popular self-named food blog (sherisilver.com), she creates and photographs recipes for numerous websites and social media platforms. You can follow her on Instagram @sherisilver.

Vivek Singh
One of the most inspiring Indian chefs of his generation, Vivek Singh has achieved global acclaim as a master of modern Indian fine dining with a culinary style that marries modern Indian flavours with Western techniques. As well as being Executive Chef and CEO of six restaurants, including Cinnamon Kitchen, Cinnamon Bazaar and Cinnamon Club, he is the author of six cookbooks, and a regular face on TV and live cookery events.

Nigel Slater
Nigel Slater is a bestselling and award-winning author, journalist and television presenter. He has been the food columnist for *The Observer* for over 30 years and is one of Britain's most highly regarded food writers. His memoir *Toast* won six awards and became a film and stage production. He lives in London.

Ed Smith
Ed Smith is an award-winning food writer and author of recipe books. His cookbooks include *Crave: Recipes Arranged by Flavour, to Suit Your Mood and Appetite*, (named Cookery Book of the Year in 2022), *On the Side* and *The Borough Market Cookbook*. He is also a regular contributor to recipe columns in *Waitrose Food*, *Waitrose Weekend*, *BBC Good Food* magazine, *delicious.* magazine and *The Sunday Times Magazine*.

Meera Sodha
Meera Sodha is a cook and food writer based in London. She has written three bestselling cookbooks, including *Made in India* (a *Times* Book of the Year) and *Fresh India* (the 2017 *Observer Food Monthly*'s Best New Cookbook Award winner). Since 2017, she has written a weekly column for *The Guardian* called *The New Vegan*. She lives in London, where she is currently working on her fourth book.

Michael Solomonov
Award-winning Israeli chef Michael Solomonov is known for his restaurants in Center City, Philadelphia. His first restaurant, Zahav, founded in 2008, received national recognition including the James Beard Foundation Outstanding Restaurant award in 2019.

Marlena Spieler
Marlena Spieler was a highly acclaimed and prolific American food writer of many food columns and more than 70 cookbooks. She wrote a number of bestselling books on Jewish cooking, including *Recipes from My Jewish Grandmother*.

Emma Spitzer
Emma Spitzer is an English chef, born and raised in Brighton to Jewish parents. After reaching the final of BBC's *MasterChef*, she has been in particularly high demand: teaching cookery classes, hosting demonstrations at festivals, catering for events and running supper clubs. She lives in north London with her family.

Rick Stein CBE
Rick Stein CBE is a chef, restaurateur, cookery book author and television presenter, best known for a love of fresh, simple seafood. He made his name in the 1990s with his earliest books and television series based on his life as chef owner of The Seafood Restaurant in the Cornish fishing port of Padstow. Since then, the group has grown to include 10 restaurants, 40 hotel rooms, self-catering accommodation, four shops and a cookery school. Rick is still at the helm with his ex-wife Jill and their three sons, Edward, Jack and Charlie, also involved. He also runs two restaurants in Australia with his wife Sarah and divides his time between Padstow, London and Australia.

Adeena Sussman
Adeena Sussman is the author of *The New York Times* best-selling cookbook *Shabbat: Recipes and Rituals from My Table to Yours* and *Sabab: Fresh, Sunny Flavours from My Israeli Kitchen*, which was named a Best Fall 2019 cookbook by *The New York Times*, *Bon Appetit* and *Food & Wine*. She is the co-author of 15 cookbooks, including three *New York Times* bestselling collaborations with Chrissy Teigen. A lifelong visitor to Israel who has been writing about that country's food culture for almost 20 years, Adeena cooks and writes in Tel Aviv, where she lives in the shadow of that city's Carmel Market with her husband, Jay Shofet. You can follow her on Instagram @adeenasussman or visit her website at adeenasussman.com

Eran Tibi
Eran Tibi (Executive Chef at Bala Baya and Kapara) is the epitome of a modern chef – high tempo, full of energy and firmly rooted in his Tunisian and Syrian ancestry. Having trained at Le Cordon Bleu and under the expertise of the Ottolenghi team, Eran now runs his own restaurants, Bala Baya in Southwark and Kapara in Soho. Both are authentic reflections of him: fun dining destinations that offer fusions of Tunisian, Syrian, Israeli and Greek cuisine, that spans a spectrum of Middle Eastern flavours.

Ofer Vardi
Ofer Vardi is the founder and Editor-in-Chief of the award-winning cookbook publishing house LunchBox Press, alongside his work as an author and editor, journalist and entrepreneur. Born in Israel in 1973 to a family of Hungarian origin, he has dual nationality and has resided in Budapest since 2017, where he offers culinary tours. In 2010, he was awarded the Pro Cultura Hungarica medal by the government of Hungary for promoting Hungarian culture in Israel after publishing a bestselling Hungarian cookbook in Hebrew (which was published in English in 2024: *Goulash La'Golesh: A Hungarian-Israeli Family Cookbook*). In 2020–2021, he wrote and edited for Foodish – the culinary department of ANU (Museum of the Jewish People). In 2021, he was named the best specialised cookbook publisher in the world at the Gourmand World Cookbook Awards.

Louisa Walters
Louisa Walters is Features Editor at the *Jewish News* and specialises in food and travel writing, plus restaurant reviews. She also runs The Restaurant Club, a social media community of 25,000 London-based foodies. Louisa has won several awards for her work in supporting the independent restaurant industry.

Joshua Weissman
Chef Joshua Weissman has been obsessed with food from an early age. When other kids were asking for video games for their birthdays, he was asking for whole

animals to butcher and prepare. Joshua began cooking professionally at age 19 and has worked at some of the top fine-dining restaurants in the United States. With his uncompromising, over-the-top approach to food, he entertains and instructs more than 20 million fans across his online platforms. He's the author of the #1 *New York Times*-bestselling cookbook *Joshua Weissman: An Unapologetic Cookbook* and *New York Times*-bestselling cookbook *Joshua Weissman: Texture Over Taste*, which was also recognised as one of Barnes & Noble's Top 10 Cookbooks of 2023.

Callan Wenner

Callan Wenner is the owner and recipe developer behind *The Cozy Plum*, a successful food blog creating bakery-style desserts, savoury bites and breakfast items, and captivating visuals that appeal to the appetites of cooks and bakers of all skill levels. Each recipe is carefully developed with thoughtfully curated ingredients and techniques, then thoroughly tested to ensure success for anyone who recreates it.

Itta Werdiger

Itta Werdiger completed a Fine Arts degree, however not understanding how she was supposed to earn an income to help support her growing family, she started cooking. She has worked in the food industry since 2007, primarily as a chef. From catering, restaurant and private chef work to teaching the culinary arts, Werdiger has cooked her ass off for many years. A visionary too, she created and ran The Hester, a speakeasy supper club in 2011, and following that, was the chef/partner at the small plates, beer and wine bar Mason & Mug in 2014. Today, Chef Itta Werdiger has gained a deeper understanding of her role with food. She says, 'My relationship with food has grown far beyond the physical dishes. I see myself as a food missionary, driven to teach and show how one can connect with the Earth, the creator and ourselves through wholesome eating.'

Simon Wood

Simon Wood is a British chef, author and restaurateur, and winner of the BBC's *MasterChef* 2015 series. He is the former chef patron of now closed WOOD Manchester, city centre. You can find him on Instagram at @simonjwooduk and swcooks.com

Shlomi Ziv

Shlomi Ziv was born in Israel and moved to the UK with his family ten years ago. He has been drawn to food all his life, thanks to growing up in a foodie family. Eight years ago, he started working in a professional kitchen and hasn't looked back since. He loves creating new dishes, but his true passion is pastry. Whether he's whipping up a classic treat or experimenting with new flavours, he always aims to bring joy with every bite. His approach is light-hearted and friendly, and he hopes his creations bring a smile to your face!

Acknowledgements

To prepare this book an obscene number of cheesecakes were made and devoured over a short period of time.

A small band of editors, along with designer Ian Hughes (who has his own cheesecake recipe included in this book), worked hard to create this second fundraising book supporting the wonderful British charity Chai Cancer Care.

First and foremost, thanks go to Kate Baker and Judi Rose, who both checked each recipe and photograph. Without them keeping this show on the road this book would not exist.

Secondly, thanks go to the other editors who also checked and re-checked each recipe. Tammy Simon, Ella Shindler, Amy Sussman, Louisa Walters and Anna Wylie all spotted and corrected numerous errors.

Laura Howard, who hosted a tasting of fourteen different cheesecakes, has worked tremendously hard to promote this book and increase the amount of money raised for Chai Cancer Care.

Finally, of course, I am tremendously grateful to Giles Coren for his foreword and to everyone who provided a recipe.

MICHAEL LEVENTHAL

Text and Photographic Credits

Baked Passion Fruit Cheesecake with Passion Fruit Curd adapted from *The New Cranks Recipe Book* by Nadine Abensur (Weidenfeld Nicolson, 1996).Photograph © Nataliia Pyzhova / Adobe Stock.

Biscoff Cheesecake by Sherry Ansky – photograph used by permission of Nicole Horwitz and Alex Levac.

Chocolate Truffle Cheesecake extracted from *Mary Berry Cooks Up a Feast* by Mary Berry with Lucy Young (DK, 2010). Copyright © Mary Berry, 2010. Reprinted by permission of Dorling Kindersley Limited.

Blueberry Cheesecake Sundae extracted from *The Bull & Last* by Ollie Pudney and Joe Swiers (Etive Pubs, 2020). Photograph © Victoria / Adobe Stock.

No-Bake Oreo Cheesecake by Martyne Burman – photograph © Victoria /Adobe Stock.

Cream Cheese and Yoghurt Cake extracted from *From the Tigris to the Thames* by Linda Dangoor (Green Bean Books, 2025). Photograph used by permission of Linda Dangoor.

Summer Lovin' Savoury Cheesecake by Aviva Elias – photograph used by permission of Michael Leventhal.

Gluten-Free Apple Crumble Cheesecake by Becky Excell from glutenfreecuppatea.co.uk. Photograph used by permission of Becky Excell.

Baked Breakfast Cheesecake extracted from *River Cottage Every Day* by Hugh Fearnley-Whittingstall (Bloomsbury, 2009).

The Ultimate Cheesecake extracted from *The Jewish Princess Cookbook* by Tracey Fine and Georgie Tarn (Quadrille Publishing Ltd, 2006).

Basque Cheesecake by Ravneet Gill: find the full recipe and more in *Sugar, I Love You* by Ravneet Gill (Pavilion Books, 2021).

Rose-Scented Mascarpone Cheesecake with Kadaifi Crumble and Candied Rose Petals by Galit Goldstein Orlow – photograph used by permission of Gait Goldstein Orlow.

Orange Blossom Cheese Danish by Helen Graham – photograph used by permission of Helen Graham.

Baked Corsican Cheesecake extracted from *Ainsley's Mediterranean Cookbook* by Ainsley Harriott (Ebury Press, 2020). Copyright © Ainsley Harriott 2020. Reprinted by permission of Penguin Books Limited. Photograph © Truprint/Adobe Stock.

Lemon Cheesecake by Angela Hartnett extracted from *The Telegraph* newspaper. Recipe copyright Angela Hartnett OBE, Murano and Cafe Murano. Photograph by Haarala Hamilton & Valerie Berry for *The Telegraph*.

Dorset Blueberry, Ricotta and Cobnut Cheesecake by Mark Hix – photograph used by permission of Jason Lowe.

Cherry Cheesecake by Ian Hughes – photograph used by permission of Ian Hughes.

Smoked Salmon Cheesecake extracted from *The Jewish Kitchen* by Clarissa Hyman (Conran, 2003). Photograph © zoryanchik/Adobe Stock.

Baklava Cheesecake by Anne Iarchy – photograph used by permission of Anne Iarchy.

Chocolate Lemon Mascarpone Cheesecake from *The Sweet Roasting Tin* by Rukmini Iyer (Square Peg, 2021). Copyright © Rukmini Iyer, 2021. Reprinted by permission of The Random House Group Limited. Photograph © David Loftus.

Parmesan and Ricotta Cheesecake from *Fireside Food for Cold Winter Nights* by Lizzie Kamenetzky (Ryland Peters & Small, 2021). Photograph by Nassima Rothacker © Ryland Peters & Small.

Vegan Cheesecake Brownies by Kirsten Kaminski – photograph used by permission of Kirsten Kaminski (thetastyk.com).

Cheesecake with Cherry Compote by Josh Katz – photograph used by permission of Steven Joyce.

Baked Vanilla Cheesecake extracted from *Tom's Table* by Tom Kerridge (Bloomsbury, 2015). Photograph © lacemika/Adobe Stock.

Lotus Biscoff Cheesecake by Sivan Kobi – photograph © Aisyaqilumar/Adobe Stock.

Ricotta Cheesecake (Cassola) reprinted with permission from *Portico: Cooking and Feasting in Rome's Jewish Kitchen* by Leah Koenig (W.W. Norton, 2023). Photograph © Serhii/Adobe Stock.

Pierre Koffman's Vanilla Cheesecake with Red Berry Compote from the Great British Chefs website: greatbritishchefs.com. Photograph used by permission of Great British Chefs.

Cheesecake, Israeli-Style by Kim Kushner – photograph used by permission of Kate Sears.

Pink Velvet Cheesecake extracted from *Vegan Bible* by Marie Laforêt (Grub Street, 2015). Photograph used by permission of Grub Street.

Cheesecake Brownies extracted from *Ready for Dessert: My Best Recipes* by David Lebovitz (Ten Speed Press, 2011), copyright © 2010 by David Lebovitz. Used by permission of Ten Speed Press, an imprint of the Crown Publishing Group, a division of Penguin Random House LLC. All rights reserved. Photograph © HUIWON/Adobe Stock.

Bobba's Cheesecake with Caramel Apples and Streusel Topping by Sharon Lurie used by permission of Sharon Lurie. Photograph © Nata Vkusidey/Adobe Stock.

Grandma Anne's Perfectly Retro Baked Cheesecake by Sarah Mann-Yaeger – photograph used by permission of *The Jewish Chronicle*.

Blackcurrant, Thyme and Goat's Cheesecake by Gill Meller extracted from *delicious.* magazine / deliciousmagazine.co.uk. Photograph by Andrew Montgomery.

Vanilla Cheesecake with Pineapple Caramel – first published in *Mexican Food Made Simple* by Thomasina Miers (Hodder & Stoughton, a Hachette UK company, 2010). Copyright © Thomasina Miers 2010. Photograph © Tara Fisher.

White Chocolate and Pistachio Cheesecake extracted from *No-Bake! Cakes and Treats Cookbook* by Hannah Miles (Lorenz Books, 2016). Photograph by Steve Painter © Anness Publishing.

South African Cheesecake extracted from *Now for Something Sweet* by Monday Morning Cooking Club (HarperCollins Publishers, 2020). Photograph used by permission of Alan Benson.

Shavuot Cheesecake Made Easy by Yanir Mrejen – photograph © Ivan Kmit / Adobe Stock.

Amaretto and Raspberry Cheesecake photograph and recipe extracted from *Jewish Flavours of Italy* by Silvia Nacamulli (Green Bean Books, 2022). Photograph by Anthony Collard.

Tiramisu photograph and recipe extracted from *Jewish Flavours of Italy* by Silvia Nacamulli (Green Bean Books, 2022). Photograph by Barbara Toselli.

Roman Ricotta Cheese Crostata with Cherries or Chocolate by Joan Nathan – photograph © Maria /Adobe Stock.

Knafe Cheesecake by Joanna Nissim – photograph used by permission of Joanna Nissim.

Honey and Yoghurt Set Cheesecake extracted from (UK) *Ottolenghi Simple* by Yotam Ottolenghi (Ebury Press, 2018). Copyright © Yotam Ottolenghi 2016. Reprinted by permission of Penguin Books Limited; and (US) *Ottolenghi Simple: A Cookbook* by Yotam Ottolenghi with Tara Wigley and Esme Howarth, copyright © 2018 by Yotam Ottolenghi. Used by permission of Ten Speed Press, an imprint of the Crown Publishing Group, a division of Penguin Random House LLC. All rights reserved.

Rose-scented Cheesecake on a Coconut Base with Berry Compote reproduced with permission from *Honey & Co: The Baking Book* by Sarit Packer and Itamar Srulovich (Pavilion Books, 2014). Photograph used by permission of Patricia Niven.

Oreo and Raspberry Cheesecake by Denise Phillips – photograph used by permission of Justyna Radon.

Vanilla and Dulce de Leche Cheesecake by Denise Phillips – photograph used by permission of Inbal Bar Oz.

Baked Cheesecakes with Blueberries used by permission of José Pizarro/Hardie Grant Publishing.

Tahini and Silan Cheesecake by Victoria Prever – photograph used by permission of Inbal Bar Oz.

Spanish Cheese Pudding extracted from *The Food of Spain* by Claudia Roden (Michael Joseph, 2012).

Citrus Cheesecake with a Kumquat Glaze used by permission of Judi Rose. Photograph © Nataliia Pyzhova / Adobe Stock.

Jewelled Mini Cheesecakes with a Cinnamon Walnut Crust used by permission of Judi Rose. Photograph © Marc Gerstein.

Rhubarb and Custard Cheesecake by Carmel Sarano – photograph by permission of Carmel Sarano.

Raspberry Cheesecake Hamantaschen by Sheri Silver originally appeared on The Nosher website. This recipe may not be reproduced without The Nosher's permission. More information about The Nosher is available on its website myjewishlearning.com/the-nosher. Photograph used by permission of Sheri Silver.

Shrikhand Cheesecake with Fennel and Coriander Strawberries by Vivek Singh – recipe and photograph from viveksingh.co.uk.

Fudgy Lemon Cheesecake extracted from *A Cook's Book* by Nigel Slater (Fourth Estate, 2021*)*. Reprinted by permission of HarperCollins Publishers Ltd. Copyright © Nigel Slater, 2021.

Honeyed Basque Cheesecake recipe © Ed Smith 2021, from *Crave* (Quadrille, 2021). Photograph used by permission of Sam A. Harris.

Vegan Baked Vanilla Cheesecake by Meera Sodha – photograph used by permission of Louise Hagger.

New School Konafi is excerpted from *Zahav* by Michael Solomonov and Steven Cook (Harvest, an imprint of HarperCollins Publishers, 2015). Copyright © 2015 by Michael Solomonov and Steven Cook. Photos by Michael Persico. Used by permission of Houghton Mifflin Harcourt. All rights reserved.

Classic American Creamy Cheesecake extracted from Marlena Spieler's *The Jewish Heritage Cookbook* (Hermes House, 2016) and *Recipes from my Jewish Grandmother* (Lorenz Books, 2012). Photograph by William Lingwood. Used by permission of Joanna Lorenz at annesspublishing.com.

Israeli White Chocolate Cheesecake extracted from *Fress: Bold Flavours from a Jewish Kitchen* by Emma Spitzer (Mitchell Beazley, 2017).

Baked Vanilla Cheesecake with Blueberry Topping extracted from Rick Stein's *Food Stories* cookbook. Photograph used by permission of James Murphy.

Eran's White Chocolate Cheesecake with Banana Compote by Eran Tibi – photograph used by permission of Bala Baya.

Strudel's Distant Cousin extracted from *Goulash La'golesh: A Hungarian-Israeli Family Cookbook* by Ofer Vardi (LunchBox Press, 2024). Photograph used by permission of Michal Revivo.

Jo's Mum's Cheesecake by Louisa Walters – photograph © AntAlexStudio/Adobe Stock.

Homemade NYC Cheesecake by Joshua Weissman.

Ube Cheesecake by Callan Wenner from thecozyplum.com.

Cheesecake de Provence by Itta Werdiger – photograph used by permission of Itta Werdiger.

Available from Green Bean Books

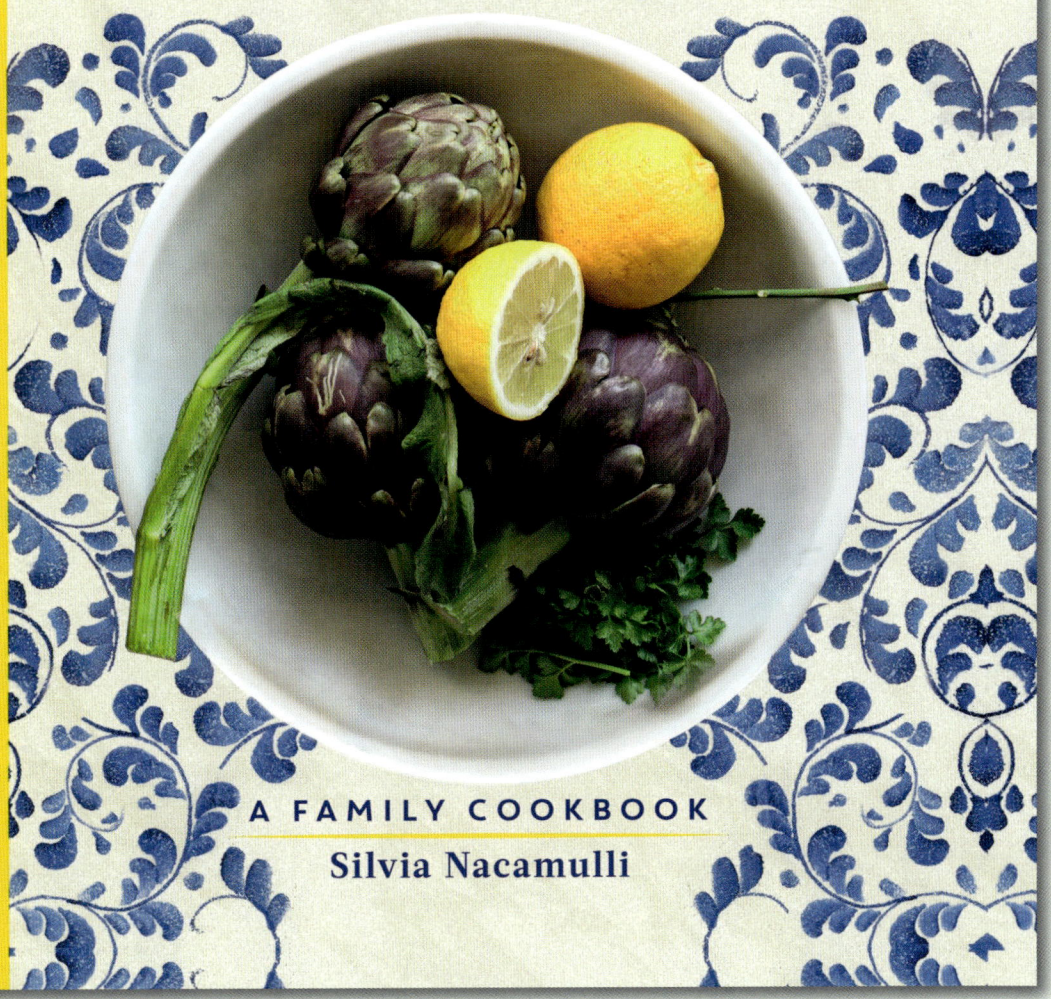

Linda Dangoor

FROM THE TIGRIS TO THE THAMES

Flavours of a Journey

A COOKBOOK